The Shameless Warrior

Victim to Warrior in 10 Sacred Promises

THE SHAMELESS WARRIOR
VICTIM TO WARRIOR IN 10 SACRED PROMISES

Published by Shameless Warrior Media
https://www.theshamelesswarrior.com

ISBN Paperback: 979-8-9913400-0-7
ISBN EBook: 979-8-9913400-1-4

Acknowledgments

I dedicate this book to my spirit brother, Lee McCormick. You inspired me for the last twenty-six years, and loved me unconditionally. You made me feel safe and protected, the way a brother protects his sister.

We have laughed in one moment and cried in the next and that has made life so sweet. I watched as you touched so many souls in their time of need. I studied as you provided them with a safe haven in which to heal their hearts. I know you are watching over me as I continue to follow my heart, love others deeply, and let my light shine bright. My gratitude to you for all you taught me and I love you brother Lee.

To all of you who feel called to read this book. I wanted to share my journey so that you can change your narrative to Warrior rather than victim. I am honored you are here, and may you open your heart fully to the personal freedom I have found from trauma. This is my journey, may you come to find reverence in the process.

Love to you as you apply the 10 Sacred Promises to your life.

Table of Contents

Chapter 9

Chapter 10

Chapter 11

Forward

by HeatherAsh Amara, author of Warrior Goddess Training and Wild, Willing, and Wise

From the moment I met Laura, I could feel her warrior spirit radiating like a gentle sun.

And just like the sun, Laura's bright spirit nourishes all those around her.

The fuel that burns so brightly in her? As she writes in the introduction to Shameless Warrior:

"I use my trauma as my fuel to continue to love in this world and be an advocate to others who have not found their voice yet."

As long as I've known Laura she has had a fierce mission to help others shift from shame to courageous, from victim to warrior. In fact, her entire life has been dedicated to healing the many layers of trauma and shame within her so she can bring the tools and skills she learned to others.

More people are speaking out about the many faces of abuse – sexual, mental, emotional, and physical. But there are still so many of us that have secret shame about past victimization and hurt. We hope we can just move through it. We tell ourselves, "Oh, but it was so long ago." But buried shame, especially from abuse at the hands of someone you love, can continue to poison us long after the experience.

In Shameless Warrior, Laura courageously shares her story and her journey to heal the many layers of trauma that developed from early childhood sexual abuse.

This is not a memoir or the individual pain of one human. This is a story that highlights the ways trauma causes us to diminish our own light and how we can reclaim it step by step.

Through her ever-deepening commitment to fully claiming her own Shameless Warrior, Laura has synthesized the healing journey into 10 sacred promises. These promises are an invitation for you to walk towards your own healing, knowing you are not alone.

Each promise, from the first Promise of Courage to the final Promise of Spirituality, shares teaching stories, questions to ponder, and specific workbook exercises.

You'll be guided by a loving hand to a self-love, respect, and joy you can't even imagine is possible.

If you are someone who carries the shame of abuse, let this book bring you back home to your own radiant, shameless warrior. The world needs your light, freed of shame and fear.

Preface

Victim to Shameless Warrior™

One of the key moments that prepared me to author this book in my life happened in 2014 when I found myself in Teotihuacan, Mexico, on a spiritual journey with a beloved mentor and healer. I was in an apprenticeship with her at that time in my life, and her name was Rita. We were in a ceremonial place in the ancient pyramids called "The Place of the Women." It is a very sacred place as there is a deep well that extends far underground and stretches underneath the pyramids. In ancient times, in the Toltec tradition, this well was filled with water.

This sacred place of the women is a strong energetic center that allows us to reconnect with the creator of our human dream here on earth. We live this human dream through our sacred bodies. When there is emotional, physical, and/or sexual trauma in our lives, we learn to disconnect from our human bodies and often live in a state of dissociation. This is a survival technique that cut us off from the pain of the trauma when it was happening so that we were able to function in the world. The problem is when we dissociate, we are not grounded and can leave our bodies, separating the mind and our heart/womb to where we are completely shut down from our feelings. This is completely normal for someone who has trauma in their background.

In the place of the women, it is a place that invites us to gently come back into our bodies and connect with our feelings and mother earth. When we can connect with our feelings and stay grounded, then we are surrendering to the truth of who we really are. Once we allow our true selves to connect with our heart/womb, whether you are a woman or a man, you will begin to feel the energetic connection and healing of the 1st and 2nd chakra, which has a disconnect due to the trauma, especially if it was sexual in nature.

This feeling of space within your heart center is the truth of who you are and allows you to be in your integrity. We go back to this place of the women to recover our integrity as it simulates the sacred womb of our birth from Mother Earth, our true mother.

I find this place of the women to be a place where I can fully surrender my human existence over to the mother and drop into my heart. It is an immensely powerful energy center for me as I can allow myself to remember when I was completely in my innocence, and it allows me to heal more each time I return. I surrender all that I am over to the mother, and she restores me back to my purest integrity during my physical birth in the human dream.

On this day in 2014, I was in an interesting place in my life. I was dealing with a lot of grief and loss in my family. The most recent loss was that of my brother Gregg, who had left this earth due to a heart attack earlier in the year. I felt immense pain around him no longer being here. I remember standing against the railing over the well. I was bent over the well, pouring all my grief and all the stories I still carried about me and my childhood of abuse into the mother herself. I surrendered all that I had over to her. I cried until I felt like I had no more tears left. This huge wave of energy began to flow out of my body and into Mother Earth as I breathed every ounce of air I had in my lungs, surrendering my heart and soul over to the mother at that moment. I felt this wave of emotion wash over me as I hung over the well, desperate to leave all my pain, shame, and loss right there with her. I found myself gasping for air. I had no thoughts in my head, just raw emotion and a feeling of surrender permeated my entire being. I took in one last breath all the way down into my womb and let out a huge sigh as I released all the air that existed in me at that moment. My body became limp as I hung lifeless in a dream state over the top edge of the well. The perceived fire at the bottom of the well had now turned to water, my face burning from the tears streaming down my cheeks.

Suddenly, I was pulled back from the scalding water at the bottom of the well and placed on the floor in front of the railing that now separated me from the well. The earth felt cool and damp against my body, and an angel stood over me, attempting to force air into my lungs. Suddenly, the air rushed into my lungs as I began to breathe again. I could sense something was different in the way I perceived the world. There are no words to describe the moment, only a tightness I felt in my solar plexus as I felt several supportive hands holding all parts of my body. My eyes were barely open, and it seemed dark around me.

I was in a conscious dreaming state as I struggled to keep my eyes open. I noticed my teacher, Rita, was smiling at me, and someone was gently cradling my head in their hands; they turned my head toward her, and she looked into my eyes. She began to speak to me slowly and softly.

"Welcome to the world, little one. We have been waiting for you. I am so happy you are here, and I love you so much. Look around you; this is your family now. All of what happened before is over. You are protected now, and you will be safe from this day forward. This is your real-life little one. Your new life starts today, and you are so loved."

There was a look in her eyes I had never seen before. I could see infinity through her eyes. I could feel her heart and a physical thread connecting us. This was a new feeling for me, and I recognized it as a rebirth and a deep forgiveness of myself in a way I had never felt before. It was profound, and I sensed my life had changed dramatically and that I would never be the same. Something had shifted in me. My life and the way I lived were about to change in ways I could only dream about. I had spent a lifetime of suffering, and today, I felt like this had been taken from me.

The women around me helped me to my feet after a few moments, and I started crying aloud, much like a child, with tears streaming down my cheeks. I felt like a newborn, just sobbing as if this were the first day of my life. They led me through a stone portal and into another room, where a ceremonial shower was performed while a prayer was said softly over me. Then, I was led over and sat down against a wall facing a portal that led outdoors. Everything seemed so new and fresh in the world as I observed life through childlike eyes. My heart felt open, and there was a sense of vulnerability as I sat still, crying aloud. I could see visions of people who would be in my life from that day forward moving through the portal, and it was so powerful to me. The visions I experienced vaguely resembled people yet had no faces, just energies about them that were authentic and filled with love. Only a few looked vaguely familiar; now when I look back on that moment. To this day, I have met some of the angels who appeared to me that day. I recognize them with my heart, and it is so endearing to me when one crosses my path. I recognize them and accept the fact that they are in my life to love me for who I am and to assist me in learning a new lesson in my life and love myself even more. Some have already appeared in my life, others have yet to come forward, yet I am sure I will be made aware of them as they are revealed to me. When the time is right, the teachers will make themselves known to me. The last one that showed herself to me in the portal that day was a short woman with long, light-colored hair. As she exited the portal, it was evident she wanted me to follow her.

This spiritual journey was five days long, and when I returned home, I began preparations to draft this book. It was time for me to share my story of how I became the shameless warrior and to outline the simple yet effective acts that you can take in your everyday life to change your narrative from victim to warrior. I have devoted my entire recovery to arrive at this point to share my sacred work with you. I know that my childhood sexual abuse was and still is my greatest gift in life. It led me to my profound appreciation of love and compassion, along with the true freedom that I only dreamed of until now. I was led to my heart and true authentic self, which I identify as "The Shameless Warrior."

I walked around for years believing I had freed myself of shame and guilt until I found out I was still carrying the shame and guilt of my family's legacy and their intergenerational trauma. I forgave my perpetrators many years ago, so I assumed that I must be done with guilt and shame. I even wrote them letters and told them I forgave them and that I was okay, and we could now get on with our lives as a family. It was true; I had forgiven them completely, and when I was around them, I never even consciously thought about the abuse again. I let them off the hook while I continued to stay in therapy for years, working through other issues that I felt were unrelated to the abuse. What I learned was everything could be related back to the trauma from my childhood, most of which was sexual, physical, and emotional.

It was only when I began working on my spiritual self that I realized that the most important person in the equation had not been forgiven. I searched my heart, and that is where I found the remnants of my family's guilt and shame, along with society's as well. There is still an unspoken energy in this world that it is not okay to talk about sexual abuse. As a society, we believe that we have made it okay to bring it up and say the words; however, we are simply paying lip service to a deeper issue. Shame runs deep in our communities, and we are still plagued by the old adages like, "Boys will be boys." Most cases are settled out of court for sexual abuse, and if they do end up in court, the men/boys are more often believed as they are not as emotional about the subject. The women/girls are left to pick up the pieces and go on as if nothing happened. This traumatizes the warrior all over again when they must relive the incident in a court of law and are once again left with no support. The same holds true for men/boys that are sexually abused and have the same experience in a court of law. They deserve the same respect of being believed and the perpetrator needs to pay for their crime.

There are certain ages when girls/boys tend to not have as much access to recall of their memories as other ages. Reports of abuse from birth to five years old are so underestimated because most children in this age range do not have an active recall of the event or the person that molested them. This makes it difficult for the survivor even to have a memory, let alone remember who their perpetrator was. In many cases, we see survivors or warriors who struggle with active recall, which will stop them from standing up against their perpetrators. The details of the trauma are not necessary. The effects are the same on each person who has survived any trauma in their life, whether it be sexual, physical, or emotional.

Because of my childhood trauma at the hands of my alcoholic father and dysfunctional family, most of the relationships I entered were toxic and unhealthy. Until I resolved the primary relationships I formed as a child in my family, I could not begin to fathom what a healthy relationship looked like, much less what it consisted of. This is a result of intergenerational trauma that I suffered unknowingly at the hands of my parents. It was passed down through many generations on both sides, a perpetual cycle of abuse until I decided to resolve and stop it. I brought to light the trauma that had occurred for many generations (consciously or subconsciously) on both sides of the family. I worked through the epigenetics that were changed in the DNA because of multigenerational abuse. As a result of my tenacity and resilience, I have changed my DNA. I have healed my wound/womb, and I have consciously stopped the abuse in further generations in my family. I have also healed the wounds of my maternal and paternal generations and the intergenerational wounds that have existed in my family for decades.

Once you begin healing your own sexual trauma from your childhood, all abuse will come out of the shadows and make itself known, and your healing will begin. I am asking you just to take small steps, as I suggest in this book. I stand beside you, holding your hand in spirit, cheering you on. Just know that you are a warrior, not a victim, and are worth loving and protecting. This is your birthright! You will learn to comfort your own little one inside and be the benevolent mother and father that you need. You will learn to listen to your child within, and that child will learn to trust you. You will learn to dialogue with your inner child(ren) and build a relationship with them. All it takes is courage. You have already survived, so the hard part is over!

As you continue to heal the wound/womb inside, you will feel validated precisely where you are and then release the shame around the sexual trauma that has been haunting you all these years. You will begin to learn to forgive yourself and see yourself in a whole new light. You will gain the freedom you never dreamed possible and begin to release the stories that you believed about yourself. This will allow you to discover your heart and fall in love with who you really are, and your world will begin to drastically change. Imagine living in this moment only and showing up for the people you love with no expectations and never being trapped by your past. You will live in love instead of fear and begin viewing the world from a new perspective. You will learn what unconditional love truly is, come to know your true heart's desire and start living by it instead of a preconceived notion that you were born into.

The best secret you will learn in this book is that the abuse, whether it was sexual, physical, emotional, verbal, or even spiritual, NEVER touched who you really were when you were born. Once you can fully grasp this, your entire life will change, and you will fall in love with life and your heart. This is the beginning of the most incredible love story you will ever come to know. Once you conquer this, your love will be reflected to you everywhere in the world!

You will find that you were born complete and will meet yourself again in your innocence, which is your authentic self. Until now, you have been in training to be reunited with your authentic self in light and love. I am offering you the same sweet homecoming I had that brought my mind, body, and spirit back in synch with my heart in this book. My life has never been the same, and I am living life with more freedom and happiness than I ever dreamed possible. I am full of love and light and live my life with integrity. I am responsible today for my actions; I think before I speak, knowing I can hurt others with my words. I do not allow others to talk down to me or disrespect me in any way. I no longer gossip, nor do I take things others say personally. If someone puts me down, it is because of how they feel about themselves. I may express my feelings in a healthy way to that person, but I do not attack them. I choose who I spend time with in my life. I align my intent with my heart and live my life with purpose according to my values and morals. I am not perfect, so if I have a difficult day, I take care of myself and go on with life. I do not spend time beating myself up; I realign my intent with my heart and continue my life in love.

The world lives in fear, which is how I became a victim. The world was afraid to hear the truth about my childhood trauma, so there was no safe place for me to talk openly about it. Once I decided I was a warrior, I began to tell the real story, and my true feelings came out. As time passed, I found people who deserved to hear my story.

To quote Brene Brown, "You have to earn the right to hear my story. It's an honor to hold space for me when I'm in shame."

I hold myself in profound honor to share your story and hold space for all of you so that I may witness your feelings.

In the act of drafting this book and addressing the trauma of "sexual abuse," I want to make it clear that this book can be used to recover from any trauma you may have experienced in life. I am a warrior of childhood sexual abuse, physical abuse, and verbal, emotional, and spiritual abuse. Just for the sake of not having to mention all five types of abuse every time I say the word trauma, I am going to address sexual abuse in the main chapters of the book. Please know that I used the same sacred promises to heal from all types of abuse.

I was so fortunate to have had a spiritual brother in my life who was safe and protective of me. His name was Lee, and he was in my life for twenty-six years before he transitioned in 2024. We had a lot of fun together, and we loved each other and accepted each other unconditionally. We had a relationship as if we were siblings, and it was so nice to experience that in my life and not have any tension between us. He taught me that life is a great mystery school. It will teach you what you already know and have inside of you. Angels appear in your life to be a clean mirror, and these people teach us so much about loving others and accepting who we really are. I must stay awake, or I will miss them along my journey of this sacred dance of life. My life has been blessed with so many people who have loved me along the way on my journey of recovery. Lee is still a great reminder to me about how important family of choice is in this world. We do not get to choose who we are born into the world with, yet we can choose our real family when we become an adult. I learned how to give up the fear by being around my family of choice that I now have in my life.

Fear drives our society by telling us how to dress, what to be, how to act, and even what is proper in the world as far as who we are, our gender, who we marry, and what is acceptable in each culture. There are those of us who are different, who may not fit the norm, who have been so hurt by society, and who are just trying to find their place.

We need to challenge the agreements we made growing up. These agreements were shaped by our parents and how they raised us, the educational system, and the government. We may have decided on our own gender or sexual orientation so that we could fit in, or we chose our career to please someone else. We may have married a specific type of person because it is all we knew. We may be afraid right now because that is what we have felt all our lives. We may be in an abusive relationship or marriage or still be at home and being abused. In any case, we can take charge of our lives and challenge all the systems that we live in, and the time is now. We need to take a good look at our agreements and make changes so that we can live our lives according to our own belief system, not one that was handed to us or forced upon us. The only way that we can begin to feel secure and protected in this world is if we take charge of our life and let go completely of what no longer serves us. This allows us to give up our attachments to the life we are living based on other people's agreements.

Once we can give up our attachments to the stories of how we have been living up to this point, then we can make room to fully surrender to a new way of living, and this brings us to our heart connection. We learn to drop from our minds into our hearts and make agreements based on who we really are, not who we believed we were, stemming from a belief system we inherited. This is when you begin to learn how to love the little child inside of you, fully and completely.

This is the love of which I am speaking. It does not mean you have to quit your career, leave where you live, or make big decisions right now. It just allows you the freedom to see your life and society from the eyes of love and not fear. Everything changes when you soften the edges of life, see yourself with love, and stop judging yourself and others. You become less critical, and instead of fear, you will begin to feel and witness the love around you.

I invite you to continue reading as we explore how to recognize the effects of trauma in our lives and how insidious a role it can play. Trauma can be hard to see sometimes when we get caught up in our careers or day-to-day activities. Learn why it is so important to address our trauma when we first identify the warning signs.

We have a responsibility to ourselves and our children to stop the legacy of childhood trauma in its' tracks so that it does not keep permeating our families.

Introduction

It is important that I share my experience of breaking the victim's mentality and becoming a warrior. I applied these ten promises to my own life and healed many lifetimes of intergenerational trauma, as well as my own trauma. I had turmoil and problems in every area of my life when I started on my journey. As I applied these promises to my life, I began to trust myself and fall in love with my inner child. I ended up forgiving my perpetrators and eventually forgave myself. This led to my ultimate healing and love of self. I became my own protector and felt safe within my own heart. I ended up with a life that was full of love and freedom.

I have always possessed the courage of a jaguar stalking its' prey. As a small child, I was held hostage in an alcoholic home laden with abuse. From an incredibly early age, I somehow had an innate sense that there was a better way to live. I developed extraordinary coping skills to deal with sexual and physical abuse that began as a toddler. It is hard to describe, though I realized I had the survival skills of someone living through a war. I developed ways to keep myself safe from harm and developed skills to deal with the pain by dissociation. I began to use drugs and alcohol to escape during early adolescence. I frequently escaped through dreaming as a young child. Even as a child in grade school, I would lay awake at night attempting to decipher and process complex dreams I had at a youthful age. Later in my life, I would learn the meaning of those recurring dreams that somehow haunted my childhood, night after night.

I was born with this iron-clad resiliency and the ability to possess a vision at an early age and to keep searching for a way to survive until I could be on my own. I had a fierce will to survive. This was part of my DNA makeup as I found the courage and strength to rise above the abuse and become a servant of love. I came to believe that the story I had lived was not mine, yet it belonged to the world, and I had to share it so others may feel inspired and know there is hope. You can overcome the most adverse of abusive situations and live a happy, loving, successful life. If I can, anyone can do it, as you will soon learn from my dire circumstances.

I have always known my destiny was to help others heal. Living this life, suffering, and being challenged to better myself prepared me to help others. I am a true example of how far a person can come by letting go of the narrative of the victim and beginning to think of myself as a warrior.

A warrior acts and keeps moving forward. I kept doing this as a young child. When I was eleven years old, it occurred to me that I needed help, so I went out on my own and found it. I felt like I had no one to turn to, so I walked into the county mental health center on my own accord and asked to see a therapist. Back in 1970, I did not have to get my parents' permission, so they accommodated my request.

I had this desire to better myself and become more aware and attempt to at least help myself and my mom, who my alcoholic father was frequently beating up at home. I came home and, being the spirited child I was, announced to my mom that our dad had a disease called alcoholism. She had never heard that word before, and I was not one to keep anything to myself, even at the expense of others. I just knew I wanted this hell to stop at home, so at eleven years old, I decided it was my duty to make it stop. Many years later, I came to learn how rare it was that I even survived all the abuse, as there were so many diagnoses ahead that I was going to have to overcome in my journey. I believe this is the reason I was born: to carry the message that we can recover and live a life of love and freedom.

The sacred promises I present in this book proved worthy of changing and saving my life. They will assist you in overcoming your trauma and seeing life from a new perspective. You are free to read the book by selecting a chapter that you relate to at a particular point in time or reading it from cover to cover. This book is meant to be helpful either way. There are workbook exercises with each chapter that are available whenever you feel comfortable addressing them. I have provided a written meditation with each sacred promise for self-reflection.

The fire that drove you to pick up this book is the same fire inside you that knows you deserve more in life, and you are ready to become the embodiment of a shameless warrior rather than a victim of abuse.

Imagine for a minute that you begin your journey today with a voice inside that is telling you that "you are loved and so worthy of this journey of the shameless warrior." Imagine that you are enough exactly the way you are and complete within yourself in this exact moment. Imagine being able to speak up for yourself and shed those old patterns of guilt and shame that were never yours to begin with. Imagine harnessing all your love and opening your heart to be present for that small child that still exists within you today. It is possible, and when you do, I promise you will never feel abandoned again.

Imagine living your life in love, not fear. You have the right to choose love over fear, and it is easy to live from love once you can be your authentic self. Imagine shedding the stories of whom you imagined or believed yourself to be based on all you were taught growing up. This is possible, and when you accomplish this, you can create a dream of what you want your life to look like.

This is your life, do not waste another minute of it. Take control now by learning how to live from your heart rather than analyzing situations in your mind. You can learn to forgive yourself and finally be free from the past that no longer serves you.

This is possible, and I have taken the same path. I am free to live in the moment, and I represent the shameless warrior. I invite you to follow the 10 sacred promises I outline in this book. They will lead you from shameless warrior in action to the true embodiment of the shameless warrior.

I base this book on my experience of my personal recovery, where my identification with the word victim kept me stuck in my story for years. Now that I look back, if someone had introduced me to the word warrior at the beginning of my recovery, I would have looked at myself and my entire life differently. I know that if we want to empower ourselves, then we can fully embrace the term shameless warrior over victim. This will enable us to identify ourselves with a stronger self-empowerment. I fully believe we can move through our issues much faster, depending on how we set the narrative. We do not have to remain stuck in our stories, and we can move much quicker into a spiritual recovery mode following the 10 sacred promises of the "The Shameless Warrior" I have mapped out personally for you in this book.

My wish for you and all warriors of trauma is that this book will lead you back to your true beloved within, which is your own heart. Your love affair with yourself will be deep and extremely rich once you find that everything you ever needed is as close as your own breath and that you were born complete.

I love you and welcome you home to your heart and your true shameless warrior.

Phone Numbers for Survivor Support Lines

Survivor Support	Contact Information
RAINN National Sexual Assault Hotline Or go to RAINN.org and click chat now to reach a counselor	(800) 656-HOPE
Sexual Abuse Crisis Text Line	crisistextline.org
National Helpline for Men who were Sexually abused or assaulted.	(800)273-8255
LGBT National Help Center Teens and Young Adults	(888)843-4564 or (800)246-PRIDE
National Dating Abuse Hotline Designed for teens and young adults.	(866)331-9474
National Domestic Violence Hotline	(800)799-SAFE (7233) or (800)787-3224
National Human Trafficking Hotline	(888)373-7888 or Text BeFree to (233733) HELP (4357)
National Indian Country Clearinghouse on Sexual Assault Hotline	(855) 464-2272 M-F 8:00 AM – 4:00 PM PST Offers Services
National Runaway Safeline	(800)786-2929
National Suicide Prevention Lifeline	(800) 273-8255 (800) 273-TALK
New Suicide & Crisis Lifeline	Text 988 from phone to reach someone
Crisis Text Line Counselor	Text HOME to 741741 to connect with a counselor

Chapter 1

Recognizing Trauma

Awareness is the first step to Recognition.

When we find ourselves experiencing a traumatic experience, whether it be sexual, verbal, or even emotional, it is easy to identify its impact while it is happening. We can experience anger, rage, depression, and even anxiety. When it ends, however, the devastating effects permeate our lives from that point on, and we can sometimes find it hard to identify the numerous lingering effects of trauma. They can be so subtle that they disguise themselves as personality traits, addictions, or a co-occurring mental illness. Any of these can be caused by and made worse by trauma, whether past or present. This book deals with sexual trauma specifically; however, keep in mind that trauma of any kind can cause the same outcome in children and adults. The details are not as important as how we implement readiness and determination when applying the sacred promises along with the exercises laid out in this book to our daily lives.

Keep in mind this book is not a substitute for professional help, which is necessary when we are experiencing somatic responses to trauma, or we have a severe interruption in our life such as loss of employment, divorce, suicidal ideation, substance abuse issues, or any addiction. We may need to consult with a therapist, psychiatrist, psychologist, or at least our medical doctor if something changes in our lives, such as sleep patterns, social patterns, or the way we deal with stressors in our everyday life, i.e.…start to panic in certain public situations, hear voices in your head that you did not previously hear. These could all be due to previous trauma you endured in childhood or as an adult and need to be checked out by a qualified professional.

Multiple studies and data reports have shown that 1 in 4 girls will be sexually assaulted by the time they are 18 years old and 1 in 6 boys. Statistics also show that 1 in 5 children are sexually solicited on the internet. The median age reported is nine years old, and approximately 40% are abused by children older than they are. 20% of children are sexually abused before they are eight years of age, and 90% of all children are abused by someone they know or trust.

People ask, why didn't the victim speak up? Often, the victims are not believed, or their life and very existence are threatened. Many, especially children, are threatened by the abuser, which means they may never tell or not tell until much later in life. These threats can include such threats as "I will kill you if you tell anyone," "I love you, and if anyone else knows, I will be taken away." The threat may also resemble, "I am doing this so you know what real love feels like," "If they find out, I will lose my job," and anything in between. A perpetrator will go to any lengths to protect themselves from being caught by silencing their warrior. This is part of their grooming process. This is part of the shame and guilt they project onto the person they are perpetrating so they can carry on and not be caught.

A key component of sexual abuse is caused by intergenerational trauma. In most cases, if a genogram is done of the family, sexual abuse or some type of trauma will be found across generations. This explains the secrecy within the family system, and this will continue until one warrior comes forward and speaks the truth about the sexual trauma within the family system. Then the secret is out, and the intergenerational trauma stops with their generation. Once the secret is out, this begins to change the epigenetics of the genes in the family, thus ending the trauma cycle. This will alter the genes in the generations to come. The warrior child, adolescent, or adult that breaks the cycle and speaks up is normally one of resiliency and tenacity and is tired of the shame and guilt they have had to carry for the family for so many generations. This warrior will heal the trauma for all intergenerations, backward and forward, in the family, and the sexual abuse will stop with them.

We have a global responsibility to clean up our ancestors' errors and our own wounds for the sake of our children and future generations. If we fail to take this responsibility seriously, we are missing the joy of our children living innocent, happy lives, as well as our children's children and future leaders. Even if there is no overt abuse in the next generation, the effects of trauma are carried in our genes, and we continue to suffer from substance abuse, addiction, and mental illness, such as depressive disorder, at the very minimum. This carries over into how we parent our children and model happiness, self-esteem, and self-love for them. By healing our trauma, we are ending the cycle.

Those of us who have experienced sexual trauma must relearn how to protect ourselves and set boundaries. We must unlearn the survival mechanisms we enacted while experiencing the trauma. We must relearn intimacy and how to have healthy human relationships.

If you have not been empowered with this information, "NO" is a complete sentence, and I am lending you my voice so that you can come forward and say it with me.

How does Trauma Manifest in our Lives?

Identifying past trauma in your life can be challenging, especially if the traumatic event occurred years ago or during childhood. Trauma often disguises itself in subtle ways, weaving into our daily thoughts, behaviors, and emotions. Here are some key signs that may help you recognize the presence of past trauma:

Emotional Triggers and Intense Reactions: If certain people, places, sounds, or situations trigger a disproportionately strong emotional response—such as anger, anxiety, or sadness, it could be a sign of unresolved trauma. These triggers can be a reminder to your subconscious of a past traumatic event, even if you are not aware of the connection.

1. **Chronic Anxiety or Depression:**

   You may experience persistent feelings of anxiety, fear, or depression, particularly if they seem inexplicable or overwhelming. These may be rooted in past trauma. Trauma can cause your nervous system to remain in a state of heightened awareness, which can lead to chronic stress or feelings of hopelessness.

2. **Avoidance and Numbing Behaviors:**

   Trauma survivors often engage in behaviors to avoid recalling painful memories or feelings. This might include withdrawing from social situations, avoiding certain places or people, or using substances like alcohol or drugs to numb emotions. Recognizing these patterns is an essential step in understanding their connection to past trauma.

3. **Difficulty Trusting Others or Forming Relationships:**

Trauma in your past, involving betrayal or abuse of power, can lead to difficulty trusting others. You may find it challenging to form close relationships, fearing vulnerability or betrayal. This can manifest as a constant sense of guardedness or isolation, even with loved ones. If you were abused as a child, you will recognize this mistrust you feel and the way it will manifest in you somatically.

4. **Physical Symptoms Without Clear Cause:**

Trauma can also show up as physical symptoms, such as headaches, gastrointestinal issues, panic attacks, or chronic pain, with no apparent medical explanation. The body often holds onto trauma, expressing it through physical discomfort or illnesses that seem unrelated to any specific condition. Children with higher ACE (adverse childhood experiences) scores typically have higher incidences of physical diseases in their adult life.

5. **Flashbacks and Intrusive Memories:**

Experiencing flashbacks or intrusive thoughts about a particular event, even if it feels blurry or incomplete, may indicate past trauma. These memories can surface unexpectedly or be triggered by a particular person, place, or movie, causing distress and discomfort.

6. **Negative Self-Perception and Self-Blame:**

Trauma can distort your self-image, causing feelings of shame, guilt, or worthlessness. If left untreated, it can lead to feelings of self-harm. You might find yourself constantly self-criticizing, blaming yourself for things outside your control or that were not your fault. You may experience generalized feelings of not being "good enough." You may have a sense of imposter syndrome.

7. **Disconnection from Emotions or feelings of Dissociation:**

If you often feel disconnected or as if you are observing your life from a distance, this could be a sign of trauma. This feeling of dissociation served as a protective mechanism, shielding you from overwhelming emotions linked to the traumatic experience when it happened to you.

Recognizing past trauma is a vital step in the journey toward healing and reclaiming your life. Trauma often shapes how we see ourselves, our relationships, and the world around us. By acknowledging its impact, you gain the power to shift your narrative from that of a victim—someone who has been harmed and disempowered—to a warrior, a survivor who has overcome adversity and is actively choosing to heal. Here is why this recognition is so crucial:

1. **Understanding the Root Causes of Your Feelings and Behaviors:**

   Recognizing past trauma helps you understand the origins of your emotions, behaviors, and patterns that may have seemed inexplicable. It can help you connect the dots between your past experiences and present-day challenges. These can include anxiety, depression, trust issues, or self-sabotaging behaviors. This understanding is empowering because it allows you to see that your reactions are not flaws or weaknesses but natural responses to trauma.

2. **Breaking the Cycle of Repeated Patterns:**

   Without awareness of past trauma, you may find yourself repeating harmful patterns, such as engaging in abusive relationships, partaking in self-destructive behaviors, or feeling perpetually stuck. Recognizing the trauma gives you the insight needed to break free from these cycles. It helps you make conscious choices different from those conditioned by your past, allowing for healthier relationships and personal growth in all areas of your life.

3. **Reclaiming Your Power and Autonomy:**
   When trauma remains unrecognized, it holds power over you, often causing feelings of helplessness or victimization. Acknowledging your trauma is the first step in changing your agreement regarding what happened to your body. Once you tell the story out loud, it loses its power over you. You realize it is only a story, not who you are. The trauma happened to my body, my mind, and even my spirit, yet it never changed inherently who I really was. You can then release the shame around the story and send it back to the ethers. At this point, you are free to reclaim the narrative of who you really are and take back your power from that moment forward. Decide how you will live your life, shift your perspective, and move on from the trauma. Ask yourself, "What can I do to heal and regain control of my life?" This transition empowers you to take steps toward recovery, set boundaries, and create a life aligned with your values and desires.

4. **Healing the Mind-Body Connection:**
   Trauma is stored in the mind and in the body at the cellular level. Once you recognize trauma, it allows you to address both the emotional and physical

24

symptoms that have resulted from your experiences. This integrated approach to healing, which will include some of the following practices: therapy, mindfulness practices, and bodywork, can help release trauma from your body, reducing physical symptoms and promoting overall well-being.

5. **Transforming the Narrative from Victim to Warrior:**
Recognizing your trauma enables you to shift your internal narrative. Instead of seeing yourself as a passive victim of circumstances, you begin to view yourself as a warrior who has faced adverse challenges and survived. This shift in mindset changes how you relate to yourself and your story. As a warrior, you recognize your strength, resilience, and capacity for growth. You will move through your recovery quicker when you see yourself as a warrior rather than a victim. You honor your experiences while refusing to be defined by them.

6. **Building Empathy and Connection with Others:**

When you understand your own trauma, this can also deepen your empathy for yourself and others. Recognizing the impact of trauma in your own life will allow you to become more compassionate toward others who have faced similar challenges. This awareness can help you build profound, authentic connections with others, creating a sense of community and support crucial for healing yourself and your community.

7. **Creating a New Future:**
Recognizing our own trauma is essential for creating a new future. When you acknowledge the past, you gain the clarity needed to decide what you want consciously to move yourself forward in life. You become aware of the past trauma and change the future for yourself and everyone around you. You can set new goals, cultivate new habits, and embrace new identities beyond the confines of trauma. This process of self-discovery and self-creation is at the heart of transforming from a victim to a warrior.

Conclusion:
Bringing up past trauma is not about dwelling on the past; it's about understanding how it has shaped you and using that knowledge to reclaim your power, rewrite your narrative, and heal your life and heart so that you may move beyond all of the adversities that trauma has caused. By embracing your identity as a warrior, you honor your journey, acknowledge your resilience, and actively choose to move forward with strength and courage. Healing begins with awareness, and with enough willingness and tenacity comes the power to transform our lives, hearts, and futures.

Chapter 2

Sacred Promise One, COURAGE

Be Brave Little One

To have courage, one must possess the ability to speak openly and honestly about what is in one's heart without fear. If one carries fear around about an incident that occurred early in life, one must be willing to speak about that trauma or secret. It must be brought forth so that one can find freedom in releasing any power that has been held in conjunction with keeping the secret/trauma buried.

There is usually a reason we keep the secret for years; it can stem from us having been threatened by the perpetrator that traumatized us, whether it was sexual, physical, emotional, or spiritual. This can be known as innate courage to be able to decipher what can be divulged of the story to survive. Many times, courage kicks in so that we can survive until we are out of the abusive situation and old enough to get ourselves to a safe place. Once we are in a safe place, we may tell the real story of the abuse or trauma. In certain cases, this is the warrior's way of staying alive by using courage to be silent until it is the right time to speak about trauma or abuse. It can depend on how old we were, when the trauma began, how old the perpetrator was, and the duration of the trauma.

Certain trauma, such as childhood sexual abuse, are less acceptable to talk about in society. Therefore, it can lead to more secrecy on the part of the child or adult. This leads to more secrets and shame, which can cause us to withdraw from life as our basic safety and security needs are threatened early on. If we, as children, have our basic needs interrupted by childhood sexual abuse, this sets us up for a lifetime of insecurity and not feeling safe no matter where we are. This is also the case when we are physically, even emotionally abused as well. The earlier the pattern of our basic needs is interrupted, the less trust we will feel in our birth family when there is trauma. Real love and security are shattered by sexual, physical, and emotional trauma early on.

Any normal discovery time spent with someone who is within one or two years of your age is different. If it is consensual and we are young children doing this innocently, this would not be considered traumatic in any way. This is simply being a typical curious child, and we should never feel shame or guilt over these incidents that are considered developmental.

If you have any questions in your own mind as to whether you were sexually abused, then I support you to go with your gut. You do not have to have a full specific memory to be a warrior of sexual trauma. Do not second guess your heart. If you have a feeling that something happened to you, then it most likely occurred. Our memory will often protect us from traumatic events in life to save our lives. Just know that if you are supposed to remember the entire event, it will reveal itself at some point in your recovery. It is possible to recover fully without the total memory of the event. We must focus on healing the effects that trauma has had on our lives and release the feelings we have carried all these years.

There may be times when you doubt in your mind whether you consented to the sex at that time and felt like it was forced on you. I am supporting you in trusting your gut and talking about it in a safe place where you can release the shame around it. You may have felt like you had no way out of it and just went through the action and never had the chance to say "no." This was not your fault. You may not have known better at the time, and now it has come up for you, and the time is right to have the courage to speak up about it. I encourage you to seek out a safe place where you can now talk about the feelings you are experiencing around the trauma.

When I look back on my life and remember my own childhood sexual abuse, there were several types of traumata happening simultaneously in my household. A violent alcoholic father was ripping my family apart, and my mother was co-dependent and just trying to survive with four children. There was verbal, emotional, and physical abuse happening at the same time. Courage saved my life as it allowed me to survive many years before I spoke about the sexual abuse I endured. I was very willing to talk about the alcoholism and physical abuse and torture of my mother I witnessed at home, though I was quiet about my sexual abuse until well into my adult years.

I had an older brother, Gregg, who was eight years older than I was, and he began sexually abusing me when I was a toddler. Since my mother was preoccupied with my father coming home and what he would do to her and us, I bonded with my brother instead of her. He paid a lot of attention to me and would corner me any chance he got. I have early memories of being in his bed with him and him teaching me how to give him oral pleasure. He would equate oral sex to something I could relate to as a little girl, such as eating an ice cream cone.

I did not understand what was happening when it began, yet he always told me, "This is our secret; you can't tell anyone, or we will get in trouble." I had no idea it was sex or anything bad, so I never told because I got a lot of attention from him. I was not getting much attention anywhere else as there was so much chaos going on at home.

Our family was a typical family in the 60s and 70s, and you would never have thought anything was going on if you looked at us. We lived in the Midwest, and my mother stayed home; our home was genuinely nice and always clean. Our father was a successful businessperson in the oil and gas industry as I grew up. We went on nice vacations as a family. They were not always pleasant, but we got to experience a lot of the country while growing up. We went to church on holidays and dressed nicely for all occasions.

We moved three times before I was four years old and ended up in a small town deep in the heartland. It was a town that was small enough so that everyone knew all the gossip that was going around. We belonged to the Country Club, and I spent a lot of time in bars as a young child with my father. He would always have to stop and get drunk before going home, as my mother had one rule at our house. "Dad could not drink at home."

The first memory I have of my life is my father being drunk and throwing dishes all over the kitchen and my mother yelling and crying. I was hiding in a closet and could see through a small opening in the door as I was silently crying. I had to be two years old. I felt terrified, and I do not remember anyone being there with me. I remember feeling alone and scared. I did not run to anyone; I stayed in the closet by myself, which shows courage from an early age. It was a coping mechanism when I was a toddler. My psyche found a way to keep me safe. I stayed quiet in the closet so no one knew I was there. What courage it took for a two-year-old to instinctively know it was not safe in their family.

I remember Gregg babysat for us often when my parents went out. Whenever he was left in charge, he would take me upstairs to molest me. He would tell our brother, who was four years older than me, Jeff, and Lynne, my younger sister, to stay downstairs. I dreaded it in the beginning, and then I began to feel special because I got so much attention from him. I never figured that they knew what was going on, as nothing was ever talked about. Of course, my parents never suspected anything, as they kept leaving him in charge of the three of us.

Gregg never molested my younger sister, Lynne, or Jeff; I was the object of his affection or the lucky one, as I felt when I was little. It became like a game to me until he began pulling me on top of him. When he had me on top of him, he sometimes would shove his penis inside of my tiny vagina, and it hurt. I would cry, and he would tell me, "Shhh, don't cry; someone will hear you." He also began telling me that if I told anyone, "He would kill me." I heard him loud and clear. He was much bigger than I was and my big brother, so I had every reason to believe that he would kill me.

I had to be around four years old when he began hurting me. Even though the molestation began much earlier, it did not hurt until this time. I began to feel confused about my feelings when the pain began. Now, love was mixed up with pain and pleasure, which really made my relationships complicated later in life. I had this anger towards him that I projected onto other people in my life, even in my everyday relationships. It made my idea of love so confusing. If someone got angry at me, then of course they did not like me, or I did something wrong. It took me years to undo the confusion of what unconditional love was from growing up with so much trauma in general.

I had so much courage, and it served me well as I would speak my mind. I can remember my mother being in labor on the couch with my sister, and I was four, and I said to her, "Well, you better bring home a girl 'cause I'm going to be a boy." She thought that was so cute, yet I was profoundly serious. I often think now, if I were a child growing up in this world where children are allowed to define themselves as non-binary or transgender, what would I have done? I have often struggled with my own gender identity and finally resolved it by simply being courageous and stating I was "gay," and when I feel like a woman, I dress as one. When I feel like a boy, I dress as a male. This has been okay for me, and I have been able to resolve my personal struggle with this gender identity crisis left over from when I was growing up.

I struggled with my safety and security in my home even though I was provided for and had everything I needed and wanted. I feared for my life from an early age. I do not remember sleeping through the night, and I have struggled my entire life with insomnia. I was on guard as a young child as I never knew when my father was coming home drunk, and he often physically assaulted my mother and verbally assaulted all of us. I was called a "bitch" or a "slut" or a "whore" before I had any idea what the words meant.

I was often awakened by my father breaking into our house instead of using his key to get in by pounding on the door so loud it would shake the whole house. I would startle as I sat up in bed, with the fear that someone was going to kill us. I spent so much time in the closet, and I can remember being shut down emotionally by the time I was seven years old. I sat in the closet, dreaming of the day I was big enough so that I could tell him what I really thought of him or beat him up to keep him off my mother.

I wet the bed every night and would get up to get my mother. This took courage, as many times Gregg would intercept me and take me into his bed, and I would lie close to him and be comforted. Then when I felt good about just being with my big brother, he would then have me perform fellatio on him or pull me on top of him so he could rub against my little body until he would cum, and then he would be satisfied. That was all I knew at the time; I had no idea it was sex. I just knew that I felt loved, and he felt pleased with me. When he was done, I was free to get my mom to change my bed and tuck me back into bed.

When I started kindergarten, I had a tough time being away from home, yet I was fortunate that my teacher was so kind and compassionate. I did not make friends easily in school and was highly insecure. I kept to myself and felt lost in the world.

My courage kicked in when I was eleven years old. My brother had gone to college, and I was lonely without him. He was now 19 years old and was the hero of the family. He was a football star at college now, playing on a scholarship. I remember going to see him at college, and we were at my grandma's house in the back bedroom. My parents had given in to my plea to sleep with him as I had missed him so much. I believe I had a lapse in memory about the abuse because as soon as the lights went out, he asked me if I remembered what we used to do, and I froze. Somehow, I had forgotten in all the excitement of just being with my older brother. I softly said, "Yes." He asked me if we could do it, and I said no.

He ignores me when I say no to his advances and rapes me as he gets on top of me after pulling me on top of him first. He is hurting me so badly, and I want to scream, but I

30

cannot. My mind is going now, asking me questions before it blacks out. Isn't this what I am supposed to do for him? I have been doing this my whole life for him. This must mean he loves me because he tells me even though it hurts. I stare out the window as tears roll down my face. My mind split into an alter ego that night to protect me, and I remember the leaves on the big oak tree outside the window that cool October night. That was the last time he ever sexually abused me.

This time, I knew better at eleven years old; I knew this was how you got pregnant, but I did not understand you had to have gone through puberty first. I never felt so lonely in my life. My parents were one room away that night; there was a bathroom in between the two bedrooms, and I was not safe and protected by them. I could not tell them. I know that I would never be believed, so my courage to face it alone saved my life that day.

When we got home, I was in so much emotional pain and felt real depression for the first time in my life. I can remember not wanting to be in this world anymore. This is when I sought help at eleven years old in therapy. I found the courage inside to walk through the door at the counseling center and ask for help instead of suffering alone. The therapist was Claudia, and she was extremely helpful just by listening to me. I remember her teaching me about self-esteem and standing up for myself. She taught me that I had a right to be in this world and that I mattered. I kept going back there, and I remember her talking to me about how brave and courageous I was at such an immature age. I started thinking, this woman is okay with me! I kept going back and talking more because she was talking about something I could relate to.

We talked about my father and his drinking, and at some point, she shared with me the 20 questions about alcohol abuse. I knew then that my father was an alcoholic. Over the next two to three years, I kept going back to counseling, and I began to have the courage to stand up to my father and tell him what I thought of him when he came home drunk. It was not always the best idea, yet at least I was speaking up for myself when he tried to attack me and call me derogatory names.

I used my courage to be discretionary about what to speak about in therapy. I never mentioned sexual abuse to any therapist. I soon found an escape to keep myself out of the house in high school. It boosted my self-esteem, which was beginning to look up if I continued to participate in therapy.

I found that participating in music and drama in high school distracted me. It provided a distraction for my mother as she came to every concert I participated in. I could feel her excitement and pride for me as well. I excelled at anything I did in music and won medals and awards in high school. I had the courage to participate in my own future and began my investment into my own future. I would not realize the depth of the effects of childhood trauma for years to come. However, I had found this amazing talent within myself that allowed me to be distracted and excel at something that became my own dream. Courage was with me every step of the way to help me survive at this time in life, and I flourished for years to come.

I became an accomplished trumpet player and vocalist, learned to play the timpani, and went to college on music scholarships. I majored in Psychology until I was a senior, at which time I received a message from an angel, "You can't help anyone until you help yourself." I had been drinking, and smoking pot and a few other drugs in the 80s, and I believed I was going to save the world by being a psychologist until I received this aha moment loud and clear.

I had the courage to listen and stay on course. I walked the line to get my BA in Psychology and stayed in school to earn a two-year degree in IT, all the while keeping up my usual music curriculum. Once I was armed with two college degrees and had proven myself in music, I set out to heal my life and begin my career, as I knew I had work to do.

I had been hiding long enough. I was ready for whatever I had to face. I knew that I had something to offer the world. I felt that I had been born into my birth family for a reason, and I was not going to waste another minute finding out what my purpose in life was.

Courage allowed me to face my shadows and take responsibility for my own life. I had dreamed about this for many years, and now it was here. I took off to California, where I began my life of sobriety and healing, developing friendships for the first time in my life.

I found a great therapist in LA who challenged me in a way I had never been challenged. I spoke of childhood sexual trauma for the first time in my life to Kathie, my therapist. I began to go to ACA meetings (adult children of alcoholics) and AA. This therapist was the first person to demonstrate what unconditional love was. She was incredible to me, and I am forever grateful to her.

I met some key people in my life who had just authored books regarding alcoholic families. I had the courage to go up to them at their workshops after they were over and ask them specific questions to understand what I heard instead of assuming what I heard. I was privileged to meet Claudia Black, PHD and go to her home at the time and tell my story of childhood sexual trauma. Claudia Black, PhD is a psychologist & author of "It Will Never Happen to Me," "Unspoken Legacy," "Changing Course," and several more books.

I believe this was the first time I told my story of my sexual abuse in public, and it was so freeing. I was validated and able to release some of my shame for the first time in my life. It takes courage to know when the time is right to finally share your story. I used my courage to tell my story in a safe place where and when I would be validated and not feel alone.

How Courage Can Be Useful in Your Life

The word courage comes from the Latin word "cor," which means "of the heart." To show courage is to speak the truth of what is in your own heart-to speak honestly and openly.

Courage is helpful in your life as it can distinguish what you say and when you say it. It allows you to use discretion to survive the trauma that you are going through at any point in your life. When you think back over your life and the events of trauma that occurred, most children, adolescents, and adults use discretion when speaking about the trauma that happened to them. You also listened to the perpetrator if they threatened you in any way.

The perpetrator is in a place of power and will use it to keep the warrior quiet during the act. This act of courage saved your life. You took the perpetrator's word that something terrible would happen to you or both of you if you called out or screamed during the act of violence or if you told someone soon after. In this case, the warrior used their self-preservation to survive the trauma or violent act and kept silent until it was safe to tell another person who could be trusted. If you survived trauma in this way, then you have nothing to feel guilty or ashamed of. You kept your body and psyche safe until your instinct indicated to you that it was safe to speak out to another person for help.

This is how we, as trauma survivors, use our courage to survive an act of abuse where we are helpless or our lives are threatened.

We who have survived trauma, especially as children, and are now facing it again as adolescents or adults will have a built-in survival mechanism that allows us to distinguish the following.

1. We must listen to our instincts and know when it is safe to resist the perpetrator or when our lives are truly in danger.

2. The ability to decipher who is safe to tell our story to that will protect us from a person who is not safe to be around.

3. We are also aware when there is danger by tuning into our gut instinct. When we follow our first impression, we find that we can always avoid danger for ourselves and others we are with.

If I could reassure you about anything, I would support you in the truth that you can always trust that your courage saved your life despite the trauma you endured.

Never believe that you were not courageous in how you handled yourself regarding when and how you trusted others. Courage is what protects you during the trauma so that you can survive it and overcome the effects later when you are able to handle them.

Those of you who have not yet found a voice to speak your truth about the trauma or violence you have endured, please be compassionate and understanding with yourself as your courage has helped you survive.

This is just the beginning of you creating a safe place within to explore, allowing your story to be heard and recognized by your heart first. Once you can write it down, you will eventually find you have the courage to tell someone who is safe and will not use your words against you. You will find the courage to speak it out loud, and it will be cathartic for you when the time is right.

Be gentle and feel your Courage in your heart with all your love.

Workbook Exercises for Courage

Think about the word Courage; what does it mean to you?

_____

_____

_____

_____

_____

Think back to when you were a child; tell about an instance when you showed Courage.

_____

_____

_____

_____

_____

How did showing Courage as a child make you feel?

_____

_____

_____

_____

Did you feel that this act of Courage as a child helped you or put you in danger then.

_____

_____

_____

_____

_____

Did you feel safe and protected as a child growing up in your home?

_____

_____

_____

_____

_____

In what way did Courage help you survive the abuse or trauma as a child or adolescent?

_____

_____

_____

_____

_____

How has Courage helped you cope with your abuse and/or trauma as an adult? Were you able to seek help on your own?

_____

_____

_____

_____

_____

Meditation for Courage

I would like you to stand in front of a mirror. If this is too much, then just sit with your feet on the floor, relaxed. Put your right hand over your heart,

Take four clearing breaths:

1. Breathe in through your nose, exhale through your mouth, and consciously let go of your day.

2. Breathe in through your nose, exhale through your mouth, and let go even more.

3. Breathe in through your nose and exhale through your mouth; on this breath, breathe all the way down to your belly and let it expand.

4. Breathe in through your nose, exhale through your mouth, and breathe all the way down to your belly. Imagine a golden light or a root from the top of your head all the way through your body, anchoring you to the center of Mother Earth.

On the in-breath, I want you to say,

"I breathe in Courage as I open my heart to love myself fully."

On the out-breath, I want you to say,

"I breathe out any shame I hold and release it to the universe."

This love you start to feel is the truth of who you really are.

Letting go of shame and giving it back to the universe will dissipate the feeling, and it will move through our body, as it was never ours to begin with. Shame is learned; love is our natural state.

I suggest doing this for 5 minutes every day. It will change the way you feel about yourself and the way you perceive the world.

When you are ready, begin to wiggle your toes and fingers as you become aware of your surroundings.

When you are ready, open your eyes and slowly look around the room, becoming aware of your surroundings.

Be aware that you can return to this meditation at any time.

Chapter 3

Sacred Promise Two, TRANSPARENCY

Moving On

Transparency means to be seen through or live one's life so those around us can see through us. It is as if we are made of glass, and the light shining through from behind puts us on display. Somehow, the light always shows who we really are when we live a transparent life, even when we try our best to hide out.

There came a time in my life when I began to be transparent. It was not until I grew up and left home that I realized the true meaning of the phrase, "You are only as sick as your secrets." I spoke about what was going on at home when I went to therapy as a young child. I was only allowing the people I trusted at that point to see part of what was really happening. I know it took courage back then to stand up and bring transparency to most of what was going on in our abusive family unit. We were existing, not thriving, and I felt like my soul was dying inside. I chose to bring enough transparency to what was happening at home to balance the amount of trauma I might suffer as I felt I had to reveal the family secrets. I had to be able to still function in school and, at the same time, be motivated to move forward in life. I decided early in life that I was going to work hard, go to college, and make sure I could care for myself and not depend on anyone. I never lost sight of these goals, and they served me well in childhood and adulthood. I know they are the reason I am still alive to put these words on paper.

I can assure you that the only way to get to the other side of the pain we are experiencing is to speak openly about what happened. Speaking truthfully about what trauma we went through and how we felt about it when it happened. This is crucial to our healing. We must walk through the fire and face the reality of what the circumstances were to get to the other side. This is where we will find true freedom and happiness. A life of forgiveness is possible once we begin to be transparent about the reality of the trauma and the effects it has on our lives today. Complete healing is possible once we begin to trust that we can live our life as a shameless warrior instead of a victim.

We need to ensure that we choose to be transparent in a safe and protected environment. It is best to check in with your heart to see if being truly transparent about your trauma will put you in harm's way at this point in your life. When you begin to be transparent about your entire story, it is best to seek out someone who can understand and support you, as your feelings may overwhelm you the first time that you tell your story.

I can look back now and see how much of my family's dysfunction lived in the open, where others could see what was going on. My father was frequently drunk in public and drove under the influence, so his behavior was not anything that others were not able to witness and take note of. His friends were all drinking with him, and those friends included the chief of police and other elected officials in this town of 30,000 I grew up in. This was all transparent to the community; they knew who this group of businesspeople were that drank excessively at the Country Club and gathered in the back of the local tire store on Sunday, as this was holy day, so the bars and liquor stores were closed.

What was not as transparent was the alcoholic who came home and frequently wailed on my mother and called his little girls every derogatory name that existed for women. He was rarely home to protect us, only long enough to cause severe damage to our psyche. His disease caused him to think highly of himself when he was out doing business or drinking with his buddies. We were left to pick up the pieces, trying desperately to help our mother as the roles were reversing quickly as she became a textbook case of an abused wife.

The world outside our home may have been aware of my father's behavior; however, it was never talked about among friends or family. My mother always put on a smile and looked good when she went out in public. However, she constantly had migraine headaches, and if my father was home, they were constantly fighting. My parents were not aware that their oldest son, Gregg, was molesting me at home repeatedly for nine years. It went unnoticed until I was ready to bring light to the subject in my family.

Being transparent at this time in my life came with a complete set of consequences in and of itself. By the time I divulged this secret, I was safe and protected and needed to tell my story to move on with my life. I could forgive all involved and eventually forgave myself in the end. This is the goal of any recovery and brings so much self-love and freedom in life.

When I was about six years old, I became extremely angry because the other kids wanted to bring light to the fact that my father was a drunk. I knew he was a drunk, and I was not fond of him at all. I had no tolerance for anyone else pointing this out to me. It was as if our family lived in a fishbowl since my father was constantly drunk and embarrassing me in public. There was a constant fight going on in our house, or my father would leave the car in neutral, and it would roll in the ditch outside, or any number of things that would indicate he was intoxicated. Just do not point it out to me; I already knew I had to live constantly as a hostage to his anger.

If another kid told me that my dad was a drunk, I would unleash on them, and my anger would take over. I would start fighting with them physically. I knew it was true, yet I did not want anyone else to ever mention it to me. It felt like I was trying to preserve my family's honor or what was left of it, even though I harbored so much disdain for this man known as my father.

I can remember feeling so vulnerable at age six. I was being sexually abused and emotionally and verbally traumatized. There was a time when a girl who was older than me put her hand down my pants. I was only six then, and I felt helpless and shocked. She began to talk to me about sexual things I had not heard of before. I felt shocked that she had done this to me, and I could not wait to get away from her. Occasionally, I would play at her house, yet I never mentioned my sexual abuse to her. I felt resentment towards her and developed this love/hate relationship with her that lasted well into my adulthood.

I could not move on from that hurtful childhood experience until I brought transparency to what happened with that young girl and acknowledged that she had to have been sexually abused by her older brother or someone in her family. No child between the ages of six and ten years old sexualizes experiences in their life unless someone shows them what sexual pleasure looks and feels like. I had misdirected my anger toward her, and I also felt connected to her at the same time. I felt like we had similar life experiences because we had both been sexually abused. She was older than me, and we never spoke about it.

My childhood was spent playing outside, and at dusk, my mother would call for me to come in. In the summer, we spent our days swimming at the Country Club until the sun went down. Then, we would all hang out in the clubhouse, playing until our parents were done drinking and socializing.

I spent time together with all the guys in my neighborhood, attempting to be just like them from dawn until dusk. Even at the tender age of four, I was determined to be a boy. I can remember a stash of Playboy magazines we had in early grade school, and we were obsessed with them in the neighborhood. I found it interesting looking at all the naked women. I loved hanging out with my guy friends and playing truth or dare with them all the time. I can remember most of the dares were sexual in nature.

If children in early grade school are obsessed with sex, then there is a problem that needs to be addressed. Children do not naturally gravitate towards sexual pleasure or games unless an adult has taught them. Today, I look back and wonder how many children in the neighborhood I grew up in were sexually abused. The statistics must have been staggering.

To be transparent is to begin moving forward with your life. As I have mentioned, I started this process early. I learned that once I told my therapist something, I did not feel alone anymore. She was safe for me and helped me deal with my depression in middle school and high school. To feel depressed at such an early age was extremely hard to comprehend in the seventies as no one seemed to talk about it then.

When I got to middle school, life changed quite a bit. I started my period and was so shocked by my body developing that I cried for six months. I wanted my mother to do anything to stop it. She swore that this was impossible. I did not want to develop breasts; I wanted to be a boy, and I was serious. I cried myself to sleep over this night after night for months. I can remember my mother taking me to the pediatrician to have them talk to me, which only made it worse. I felt embarrassed and was adamant I wanted to be a boy.

In middle school, we had gym class separate from the boys, and we had to put on this one-piece outfit for gym and shower afterward. I wanted no part of it, and it was extremely traumatic for me. I was ashamed of my body and did not want anyone to see me change. I especially wanted to avoid taking a shower in front of anyone. Girls could be mean, and it hurt my feelings when someone would laugh at me for any reason. I was extremely sensitive to what other people thought of me, and I was extremely self-conscious due to the trauma I was being subjected to. I was not a popular kid at school and was extremely introverted at this time in my life.

I was known for making everyone laugh in class, and this resulted in repeated parent-teacher conferences and me getting detention. I was okay with it as I did not like being at home at all. I tried to find more excuses not to be home as I could not stand being around the chaos and terror that was going on at home. My brother Gregg had left for college, and it was now just me, my sister, and our other brother. There was more violence going on at home as my father seemed to be coming home in the afternoon drunk and causing more problems. I was not strong enough to keep my mom safe. I was checked out emotionally and probably dissociative by this point.

My homeroom teacher, Mrs. Davis, just adored me, and she picked up on the fact that I was a troubled child. I somehow found myself in detention more often than I care to admit, yet I loved spending time with her. When we were alone, she would say things like, "Laura, I love you like my own" or "You really are a good kid." I could tell and feel that she really did care about me. I can remember writing her a letter of gratitude at the end of the school year in seventh grade. I went to see her that summer at her house, and she had my letter underneath the glass on her coffee table. She told me it was there because she cherished it. I can remember a warm feeling when I saw it and when she hugged me that day.

I asked her if she would be back for eighth grade, and she told me she was going on a long cruise. I knew something was not right about that answer, yet that was all she would tell me. I hugged her, but I never saw her again. Later that year, she died of cancer. I suppose she did not have the heart to tell me the truth. I remember being devastated, yet I did not show any emotion. I could not process this as she genuinely cared about me, and now she was gone. I had not lost anyone close to me, so I did not know what death was all about. In some ways, this reinforced the fact that if someone cared for me, they would leave.

In eighth grade, I had a new gym teacher. I remember being more transparent about how I felt about my body with her. She was young and became like a big sister to me, and I began to trust her. I even went to church with her and her husband, Vern, a few times. I admit that Beth was the most positive influence of anyone in my young life. My attitude began to look up for the first time. Beth was there for me when I needed someone that I could trust who really cared deeply for me. She was the first person that I could call on when I needed help, and she would be there for me.

Transparency saved my life when I was willing to share some of what was happening to me. I shared just enough to get the help I needed to cope until I could make my dreams come true. I knew I was going to be free of all this once I went away to college and I could finally live my life fully.

Once I was out of danger, transparency was freeing in many ways. Discretion is a survival mechanism survivors use to create safety. I would have been beaten had I fully disclosed what was happening at home as a child. I wanted to be able to function and still be able to fulfill my dreams. The best way I knew how to survive was to become involved in music and drama and be away from home as often as possible. This worked for me as a great distraction and shaped my values as a child growing up. It instilled in me a sense of work ethic that I took into my college years. I was successful at putting myself through college by succeeding at music.

Transparency has allowed me to heal from my trauma and gain the freedom to be openly honest with myself and others. I have released myself from the pain that my sexual trauma caused me in my childhood and into adulthood. I have been able to feel the pain, walk through my feelings, and make new decisions about what happened to me. I no longer ask questions regarding why this happened to me. I use my trauma as my fuel to continue to love in this world and be an advocate to others who have not found their voice yet.

Transparency has set me free and allowed me to return to who I have always been. My heart is full of love for everyone on this journey. Recovery is possible.

How Transparency Can Be Useful in Your Life

The root of the word transparency comes from the Latin root transparentem which means "see light through." To live in a glass house.

When you look back at your life, you will find that being transparent was not always possible during the times when your trauma was taking place. You were so focused on survival that transparency might not have served you then.

You may not be capable of being transparent about the trauma, and that is okay. No one should rush you until you feel comfortable and safe. It is so important to surround yourself with others who love and support you no matter how you feel as you tell your story for the first time or the tenth time.

Transparency may not all come at once. Lapses in your memory may not allow you to share the entire incident in one setting. If you were traumatized in any way, know that you are a survivor or warrior. Even if the threat of trauma was perceived and you are suffering the effects today that trauma can cause, pay attention to your heart, and know that you are a trauma survivor and you are a warrior, not a victim.

The experience of trauma, whether it be sexual or physical, could have been preverbal. If this is the case, then the memory will be cellular and may come out in actions rather than words. Regressive therapy is just as powerful as recounting the trauma from memory as you will find that your visceral memory is very real, and there can be a powerful release through somatic healing.

There are workshops that can help you be supported in bringing transparency to your trauma, and you will not be judged during the experience. A group will assist you in bringing your voice forward and holding space for whatever feelings may come up. There will be no judgment in the workshops, only acceptance and unconditional love. You will be victorious in identifying with being a warrior instead of a victim!

When you are ready, you can use the exercises in this book to help you bring light to your trauma and experience them for the first time. If you feel overwhelmed, see the list of phone numbers at the front of the book and contact one of the organizations listed for professional help.

One must be transparent with themselves to get to the other side of the pain. It is essential to acknowledge the trauma that occurred, work through it, and look at the story around all of it. We all tell ourselves stories about the trauma and how it happened. The truth is, it is a story that damaged our bodies, minds, and even our spirits, yet it never touched who we really are. Who we are is so much deeper than a story of what happened to us. Who we are existed before we came into this life, and the truth is that we can change our stories anytime.

We made agreements early on in life about what we were going to believe about ourselves and our parents and what we believed we were supposed to act like based on all the input from school, parents, and even social media. The truth is that these agreements were influenced by everything and everyone around us as children.

Now, we are grown, and once we become transparent about what happened to us as young people, we can shift our attention to the agreements in our lives and whether they still serve us or not. We must look closely, and then we can change the agreement to the present day. We are free to be whatever and whomever we want to be. We can develop our own values and raise our children the way we want to. By changing our agreements, we are free to create the life we have always wanted to have.

When we change our agreements and become transparent about our lives and the trauma that occurred, we begin to clear the legacy for our children and for many generations to come. Once we do our trauma work to heal our wounds, we clear our ancestral wounds so that those who come after us do not suffer any longer from the trauma that was passed down.

To be transparent is so important to healing our wounds/womb as the abuse we suffered as warriors caused a disconnect between our 1st and 2nd chakra. This is our root chakra that grounds us to the earth and our womb chakra which gives life. At some point in our healing, we must acknowledge all our conscious memories and cellular/visceral memories so that we may clear our bodies of the energy of the trauma.

What can be put in place of the trauma are new agreements we can make with our bodies, minds, and spirits that support us in a free, healthy, loving way. We can also change our stories about who we are or aspire to be and begin living heart-centered lives that fully serve who we really are. At this point, we will recognize our true heart's desire and realize how much love is in us and the universe. When we love, the world will love us back, and we will see ourselves everywhere.

Thoroughness in your transparency will bring about love and freedom for your own self, sparing your children the guessing game of what really happened in the ancestral family they were born into. We now have the strength and knowledge to clear the trauma of seven generations by facing the fears brought forth in our lives and releasing the shame around them. At this point, you will be able to move from victim to shameless warrior once you release the old story of who you were and take charge of your new story of who you really are in this place of freedom and love that you will come to know as your own heart's desire.

Workbook Exercises for Transparency

When you think about Transparency, what comes to mind?

_____

_____

_____

_____

_____

Has Transparency been helpful at any time when speaking about your abuse?

_____

_____

_____

_____

_____

Have you always been Transparent about your abuse? If "yes," with Who? If "no," Why not?

_____

_____

_____

_____

_____

Write down a story you believe about yourself because of the trauma from your life. For example, my dad constantly beat me up as a teenager. Therefore, I cannot trust any relationship with other men.

_____

_____

_____

_____

_____

If you were to re-write the agreement to the question above, in your mind, what would you like it to say? We have the power to change our agreements in this life at any time.

_____

_____

_____

_____

_____

Write down anything about your life that you have yet to be truly transparent about with anyone. (This is between you and the paper; I welcome your courage and feel free to write your feelings about divulging it also)

_____

_____

_____

_____

_____

Meditation for Transparency

Get comfortable, preferably sitting in a chair with your feet on the floor.

Place your right hand over your heart and left hand over your womb (lower stomach area).

Take four clearing breaths:

1. Breathe in through your nose, exhale through your mouth, and consciously let go of your day.

2. Breathe in through your nose, exhale through your mouth, and let go even more.

3. Breathe in through your nose and exhale through your mouth; on this breath, breathe all the way into your belly and let it expand.

4. Breathe in through your nose, exhale through your mouth, and breathe all the way down to your belly. Imagine a golden light or a root from the top of your head all the way through your body, anchoring you to the center of Mother Earth.

Now breathe in and concentrate on your hand over your heart; feel your heart open further to love in the next four breaths. Think or say aloud, "I open my heart more to the love in the universe," on the in breath.

Now, on the exhale, think or say aloud, "I breathe out any resentment I am holding in my heart," keeping your hand on your heart for four exhales.

Shift your attention to your womb; the next four breaths in, "I open my womb to begin to heal my trauma," and then on the exhales, "I breathe out any obstacles that are blocking me from healing."

You can repeat this exercise as many times as you would like until you feel your heart open or soften and your womb soften.

Chapter 4

Sacred Promise Three, TENACITY

Staying the Course

Tenacity means to have courage in the face of danger to stay the course even in times of extreme difficulty. There is a spirit associated with the word tenacity that suggests that a person can hold on to their principles and keep up their morale when threatened. Tenacity represents a determination to stay the course until one's resolution is achieved-a person who will not admit defeat.

When I look back on my life, tenacity was necessary for my survival. When I was a young child, there were so many times that I feared for my life. I had no control over any of my surroundings from the day I was conceived. I was held hostage to whatever was going on around me, and it was caused by my parents. When I was born, I had two brothers, so my nuclear family consisted of five, and it was utter chaos. I know that I was determined to change my life early in grade school, yet before that, the damage had been done to me. My neuropathways were already programmed for a life full of hurt and trauma. I had been abused in every way there was, sexually, verbally, emotionally, and physically; however, there was still a fire somewhere that knew I would survive and rise above and make it out alive.

At the time I was born, my father traveled for work, so he was gone a lot. He was already deep in his infidelity and drinking. My mom had three small children and no one to turn to. My parent's generation was known as the silent generation, and people did not talk about their problems. They had grown up during the depression, so this time of financial security and the ability to live a stable life was long overdue. The women still had little rights and no credit of their own. There were a lot of stigmas around getting a divorce and being a single mother, and if a woman were to divorce, finding a job and supporting her children would be almost impossible. Women stayed married, even if they were miserable, for the sake of their children.

My mom was depressed when I was born and for as long as I can remember. My father did nothing to help her. He just went to work and came home when he felt like it. The absurdity in my house could be demonstrated by the fact that my mother refused to cut my father's birthday cake until he came home. Fast forward three days, and we finally got to cut the cake amidst the fighting. However, we were desensitized to that. The fighting had become a background noise in our everyday life. My father's rants and severe alcoholism grew increasingly more frequent as I grew into an adolescent.

We became a family of four children, all four years apart. I watched my mother grow more tenacious as her girls grew up. She was determined that we were going to be stronger than her and never let a man push us around. I grew up to a constant barrage of her repeating, "Don't ever let a man lay a hand on you," or "You get your education so you can take care of yourself and leave anytime you want to." I became stronger and stood up for myself using my courage. I was not concerned about the outcome but determined to regain my power. She was a small woman, however, the strongest woman I have ever met. She always had the energy to make sure my little sister and I had what we needed, and we felt like we mattered in this world. She was just too worn out to be available emotionally and for that, I forgive her. She absolutely did the best she could, and I got my strength and courage from her.

I never felt like I had anyone I could talk to as I was the oldest girl. I did not fit the role of a big sister and wanted to have a big sister figure in my life when I was little. Soon, my older brother, Gregg, was sixteen, and I was eight, and he began bringing home his girlfriends when he would babysit. I was so thrilled to have someone who was female and older around me. At this point, he had sexually abused me for at least seven years, yet I longed for a big sister. I would sit on his girlfriend's lap and demand their attention, and they seemed to enjoy having me around.

When the sexual trauma begins incredibly early in life, and you grow up with your perpetrator, the lines between trust and safety become blurred. I felt a sense of loyalty and a special bond with him. He seemed to always look out for my well-being. If I failed in life, then he would feel guilty because he had sexually molested me. He carried shame around about what he did and would make sure that I was succeeding at what I was doing. I know this as he would express his opinion if something was not going well for me.

As you get older, the sexual trauma interferes with any relationship you attempt to have as you quickly project unrealistic expectations of what your perception of love looks like onto the other person. I knew for myself it was impossible to enter any romantic relationship until I truly resolved my feelings about my brother and forgave him. I then had to work on self-forgiveness, and that is when I became capable of entering a healthy romantic relationship. It takes time; however, it is the best thing you can do for yourself.

My brother Gregg had many friends who were guys, yet I was never happy to see them. I was trafficked out to them in our house by my brother. I had no say in this situation at all. I was afraid of my brother, as he groomed me to keep me loyal to him. I was afraid to say no to him because I did not want to disappoint him. He would have me hide behind the bathroom door, and then he would tell one of his friends to come in. Once they came in, he instructed me to perform oral sex on them. It seemed like a game, and I was eager to please my brother, so I did whatever he wanted me to do.

It seems so sad to me now when I see that little girl inside of me and what she had to endure. When a child is abused at such an early age, they become very vulnerable, and their innocence is stolen away from them forever. Older boys constantly preyed on me, and it did not matter where I was; I was continually approached for sex. I assumed if I tried to say no to them, there would be some kind of consequence far worse than the act of sex itself. I rarely got attention except for the strange sexual encounters I was approached about, so I thought that was why I was here: to satisfy these older guys. I very rarely turned down the sex as it fulfilled some sort of self-worth in me. I was not clear what else my role was until I could get out of the house and begin to understand the effects the trauma had on my life and the way it had shaped me and my personality.

My extended family lived about sixty miles away from us, and we would visit on weekends. We had so much fun growing up close to our first cousins, and I always felt safe with my aunts, uncles, and grandparents. I can remember the depression that would set in on Sunday when we would have to come back and the desire to secretly go live with them. I even asked my mom if we could go live with them. She always said she could not just leave with four kids and no job. I understand now, but I had no sense of her reasoning as a child. I just wanted that experience of feeling loved and protected that I did not feel at home.

Because of the trauma I was enduring at home, I spent as much time alone as I could. I had no close friends and, due to stress, was in a lot of pain emotionally and, at times, physically. I had so much time to build up tenacity and ensure that I stayed the course. The older I became, the more time I spent in my room. This is where I discovered music, and it became my life and escape.

My home resembled a war zone. When my brother Gregg was still at home, and my father would come home drunk and start hitting my mother, Gregg would physically throw my father off my mother when he attacked her. Then, a physical fight ensued between my father and Gregg until all the furniture was out of place, and my father was defeated on the floor. It was like having a live wrestling match in the family room. I would watch from the stairs, of course, listening to all the obscenities being tossed around. Then Gregg would leave, and inevitably, there would be broken glass somewhere. My mother would cry; it was just chaos all around. This seemed like a nightly occurrence for most of my childhood.

My father left for the last time when I was a senior in high school. The four of us children came together and announced to my mother that we were done. We made the decision that he would not return to our home. We knew if we had let him come back, he would have eventually killed my mother. He lost his business with Standard Oil and embezzled hundreds of thousands of dollars drinking at the bar across the street.

He never went to jail. Our family had friends in Standard Oil who did not want to see my mom, with four children, have her husband in jail, so friends of the family in top management of Standard Oil kept him out. Everything that my mom sacrificed for was gone: his pension, insurance policies, any stock, and the house went into foreclosure.

My parents finally divorced, and he refused to pay any child support. My mom, sister, and I moved sixty miles to where our extended family was, and I began college as a Psychology Major and Music Minor.

College was great for me. I proved to be incredibly talented in every musical group I participated in on campus. I was on my way to being a psychologist, which had been my dream since I was young. I began dating for the first time and lived a gay lifestyle. I felt free to be who I was and began to have fun for the first time in my life.

After I graduated in 1983 with two degrees, a BA in Psychology and an AAS in Information Technology, I pulled my first geographic and moved all the way across the country. I moved to Los Angeles with the idea that my life was really going to begin in a big way. I would have no one to answer to, and I could party as much as I wanted.

I was living in West Hollywood in the '80s and having a wonderful time until reality set in that I was still here. I had come all this way, yet my mind would not leave me alone. I did not survive long without therapy and found my way back after six months. I had just displayed the tenacity in my life by getting myself out of the war zone, through college with two college degrees, and back in therapy, asking for help when I needed it. In six short years, I had done so much that I was not about to give up at this point. I asked for help, and this time, I was out of ideas because this was the part I had no idea how to navigate. I was on my own trying to start a career 2000 miles away from where I grew up. On top of that, I was still active in my addictions and lonely. This time, I was ready to listen, put in the time, and begin to get serious about my life.

As synchronicity lined up, I found my way to this incredible therapist, Kathie. As fate was on my side, she knew about Adult Children of Alcoholics. There were meetings I went to where I learned that all the craziness I was going through in my head was not my fault after all. My father had been the problem all along. Such a weight lifted off my shoulders, and then I concluded that I was not crazy; it was my father!

My use of alcohol and drugs was progressing during this time. My therapist, after about six months, suggested that I might try out some AA meetings. There was a conflict inside of me. I knew I had a problem with alcohol, although I was not ready to face it. I was afraid to find out what I was medicating if I stopped drinking. Would I survive the feelings if I stopped? These are genuine concerns for anyone who has an addiction, and I had been working on my issues of trauma for a few years, so I was wide open when I found myself in AA meetings. In those days, we raised our hands in meetings if we identified ourselves as alcoholics. It took me a good six months to raise my hand after a rough bottom to my drinking and drugging that resulted in me paying an emotional price, which left me depressed once again.

I continued to drink and attend open meetings for several months before I admitted I was an alcoholic. My last drunk was destructive and reckless. I was living in the San Fernando Valley at this point and went down to West Hollywood on a blind date. We arrived at a party, and there was marijuana and heavy drinking going on. How could I refuse? This girl had a hot car, and we were at a party in my favorite party spot, where alcohol was flowing, and weed was readily available. It was not long before we were both wasted. I knew that the program messed up your drinking, but I was determined to have a fun time. I dissociated to the point where I was on the ceiling, watching myself drink and smoke weed. My subconscious was even talking to me as I kept smoking the weed, and I was already higher than a kite. I knew better, yet I continued to take hits from this joint until it was gone. You can only get so high; however, the point was I could not stop myself. I kept drinking also, and I was observing myself from above, and I could see my addiction in action. I became scared because it was at this point I knew I was an alcoholic and an addict. I asked the girl to take me home. She proceeded to drive me home, and she was intoxicated as well. This was the first time I had been afraid for my life as I observed her running a couple of red lights.

I made it home and just cried; I could not wait to go to a meeting in a few hours. When daylight broke, I called a friend from the other program of Adult Children of Alcoholics and asked where the closest meeting was. I went there early that morning, raised my hand that I was an alcoholic, and took a surrender chip. I was finally defeated enough to fully surrender to this way of life.

Tenacity has been vital in me hanging in with AA for a few 24 hours, as we say in the program. These add up to years of sobriety and staying clean. My sponsor in California was no less than an angel sent to rescue my broken soul. I was willing to listen and work the steps exactly as I was told. This was a very tough part of my life; however, I was finding my way through my feelings for the first time. I began to realize how I used my addictions to cover up the hurt, sadness, and shame I had carried with me in my life since I was born.

Staying the course has resulted in my recovery from the trauma I had suffered since I was less than two years old. I dared to face my fears and kept working the twelve steps until they began to work for me. I knew that I had everything to gain by moving forward through my pain, and there was a plan for me that was bigger than I could ever imagine in this world. I knew that there were so many other people who suffered as I had from trauma, whether it was sexual, physical, emotional, or verbal. Just take your pick. It does not matter; it all results in the same response for each of us. By the time I was in my thirties, I knew for certain that my story was not mine; it belonged to the world. I knew the world needed to hear my story one day so that others could find their voice and know there is freedom once you do the work and overcome the aftermath of your trauma.

How Tenacity Can Benefit You

Tenacity is "determination; the quality of being determined to do or achieve something. Not giving up."

When you scan your life, think of when you were young and were told "no" about something you wanted to do that was important to you, and you did it anyway. Chances are there were times that you persisted, which changed your life trajectory. In these situations, you were determined to do something that you felt was the best action for you to take at that time in your life.

Tenacity allows us to overcome trauma, and persistence will enable us to break the mold for the next generation. Any time we work on our trauma, it also heals the collective trauma in the universe. This helps the current and next generations heal and will raise the vibration in the world in which we exist.

The people around us who are still acting out their trauma on their children or grandchildren are operating at a low vibration. Their energy is toxic, and they need us to work with our tenacity to help set an example of how we can be kind and loving to our children and the next generation so that we can stop the cycle of abuse. It is possible through our actions that others may follow our work and begin to stop their cycle of trauma. They may like what they see in us and want to live in this higher vibration or frequency that we create by taking our personal journey toward freedom from past trauma.

When you persist with tenacity in your life, you realize that you have survived childhood, adolescent, or adulthood trauma, and you can stand tall in your own recovery from your past. You are now chosen to seek out the support you need to keep moving forward through the pain and make new decisions about your life.

Approach your healing from shame, name it, feel it, put it outside of yourself, and then release it to the ethers. Once you feel the feelings of the original trauma that happened to you, then you can look at it as a story of what happened and make a new decision of who you really are.

Using tenacity, you can author a new story about your life and bring your wisdom forward with you from this day. Walk into a new future, never let the past rule your life again. It is possible. I have been there and can promise you that life can be heaven on earth when you do your inside work.

Never give up on happiness and freedom, as it is accessible no matter what trauma you have in your past. It might not feel easy at times when you are going through your recovery in therapy or addiction rehabilitation. Whatever the case may be, it will be worth it.

Once we are honest with ourselves about what happened in childhood, we can move forward. We need to decipher who is safe and who is not, and sometimes, we learn this by tuning into our gut and listening to what others are saying. Once we begin to learn about boundaries, it will be easier to decipher who is safe in life. This will make it more accessible to find others with whom to share our story.

Once we learn to treat ourselves and the little ones inside of us lovingly and with kindness, we will be better equipped to choose others worthy of hearing the stories of trauma we endured. This often encourages others to open up, and we can begin to support one another through the pain. There are so many of us who have gone through trauma in our lives, so remember that when you are approaching other people. Once we know that we are not alone, this helps us to find one another through twelve step groups or support groups in general.

Just be gentle with yourself as you work through the trauma from your childhood or any part of your life. Always remember that working through any trauma will improve your life immensely and bring you the freedom to fully grow into yourself.

Workbook Exercises for Tenacity

After reading this chapter, what does Tenacity mean to you?

_____

_____

_____

_____

_____

Can you see how Tenacity helped you survive trauma in the past?

_____

_____

_____

_____

_____

What does letting go of shame feel like for you?

_____

_____

_____

_____

_____

Are you willing to break the cycle of abuse for future generations by doing your own work?

_____

_____

_____

_____

_____

Are you aware of what a safe person is? Are you willing to write about what traits they might have?

_____

_____

_____

_____

_____

When you look at your life, can you see yourself in a life beyond trauma?

_____

_____

_____

_____

_____

Do you have a therapist, or have you had someone that you can trust with your feelings who can help you move beyond your trauma?

_____

_____

_____

_____

_____

Meditation for Tenacity

Find a place that is quiet where you can sit comfortably.

Take four clearing breaths:

1. Breathe in through your nose, exhale through your mouth, and consciously let go of your day.
2. Breathe in through your nose, exhale through your mouth, and let go even more.
3. Breathe in through your nose and exhale through your mouth; on this breath, breathe all the way into your belly and let it expand.
4. Breathe in through your nose, exhale through your mouth, and breathe all the way down to your belly. Imagine a golden light or a root from the top of your head all the way through your body, anchoring you to the center of Mother Earth.

Now close your eyes and keep breathing slower as you begin to picture yourself at a certain age in your mind; this could be when a particular trauma happened.

Keep that little girl or boy in your mind, still breathing; take note of where they are, what position they are in, what they are wearing, and whether they are happy, sad, or angry.

Keep breathing and see if your little one will allow you to come near them. Ask them and see what they say. Keep in mind they may be pre-verbal, so you may have to notice cues as you move closer (if they do not allow you to approach, stay at a distance).

Still breathing, if they allow you to come near, just slowly walk near them. If you can ask them how they are feeling, allow them to tell you. Listen to what they tell you about their feelings. If they are willing to tell you, let them know you are always there for them. Stay at a distance that is comfortable for them. Just observe them and how they react to you.

After spending a few minutes, tell them you will be back to see them and that you are always with them. Observe their reaction to this. Walk away a little in your mind and stay closer than when you began this meditation.

Still breathing into your womb, ground yourself, and know that it is okay if your little one has tears, and you may have tears in your eyes as you say, "So long for now." It is OK to feel sad or hurt. Emotions are fluid, and they will pass through us.

When you feel grounded, put your right hand on your heart. You can slowly open your eyes and softly gaze at something in the room.

Keep your hand on your heart. Remember the little ones you just visited with and know that they are always in your heart.

You may want to write about this meditation or draw a picture of your little one or how they felt.

Feel free to repeat this exercise as often as you want. You can also move closer to your little one if they allow you to. You may even hold them, touch them, or hug them, depending on how they feel about it. Always tell them you "love them" if you can and let them know you are there for them now.

The idea of this work is to become your own benevolent mother and father to your little ones inside who were abandoned during your trauma when you were a child. It takes a lot of work, and you may want to find a therapist or a safe person who understands this type of work to practice this meditation with.

Chapter 5

Sacred Promise Four: RESILIENCY

Trait of a Warrior

Resiliency means having the ability to recover from any misfortune in life or even illness quickly. People associate toughness with resiliency; however, it is the capacity to withstand difficulties in life and pick up and go on regardless.

Now that I am an adult and look back on my childhood, I can see that I would make light of dire situations by being funny. That was my redeeming quality. I have always used humor and still use it to this day to make others laugh. The difference today is that I have worked through most of the abuse and trauma that I suffered at the hands of others, and now I can find humor in some of the stories that happened to me when I was young. They are not funny, and I would never laugh at anyone else's circumstances surrounding their trauma.

I find the absurdity of the adults who oversaw our household comical at times, now that I have overcome the pain around the truth of what really took place. It was a coping mechanism when I was going through the original trauma until I could find a safe place to relive the trauma and feel the feelings that I hid as a child. I was the mascot in the family, and I never shed that role. I did take my recovery extremely seriously and sought help as soon as I could, and, at times, I even felt depressed around the trauma, working through the issue of co-occurring mental illnesses over the years.

I was resilient as a child and never allowed people to see me down. I always knew a better life awaited me, and I was determined to find it on my own. I knew I was living through this hell for a reason, and one day, I would escape it and live my life the way I wanted to. I spent so much time alone as I got older and had so much time to plan my future when I was not performing in music activities.

Using music to escape the hell I was forced to live in, I would go on to college and earn a music scholarship in my junior year. This was a goal I set for myself, and I attained it. I earned a music scholarship to attend SMU in Dallas, and I was the first girl to play trumpet and receive a scholarship in the famous SMU Marching Mustang Band. I remember feeling so proud of myself for accomplishing this on my own. I was tenacious when it came to my music. I was also the first girl to play first trumpet in the SIU Marching Salukis. I always set many goals and achieved them in high school, college, and after I went to California. This always kept me on track and hungry to keep on the task of my recovery.

During my alone time, I learned to entertain myself. When I was in my early teens, I watched Carol Burnett every week and laughed so hard I could not breathe. I would tape the show on a small cassette recorder to play it back during the week and laugh at all the scenes as I recounted them in my mind. She was my idol and got me through so much trauma at home by providing me comic relief. I had the chance to tell her this story a few years ago when I found myself in the front row at one of her talks. I told her how she saved my life when I was a kid by allowing me to laugh at her show all week long as I listened to her repeatedly on my little cassette recorder. I told her she was my Shero growing up and that, rest assured, she saved this little girl's life somewhere in the Midwest, laughing hysterically at her show, knowing there was a better life waiting for her. She gave me hope, for sure, as a child. She appreciated hearing the story, and the entire audience erupted in applause. I still have a picture I received from the studio when I had written to her as a child many years ago. It is one of my most cherished childhood memories, receiving that picture.

I always demonstrated resiliency in school. No matter how bad it was at home, I still had school to escape my abusers. I was not the best student, nor was I the most well-behaved. I knew how far I could go before getting into serious trouble. So that is how far I would push my teachers.

All the therapists who worked with me told me they enjoyed working with me as I worked hard to overcome any obstacle. No matter how painful, I was willing to do the work necessary. I just knew there was a better way to live if I hung in there. If you look at my pictures, I was not always happy; there was no sparkle in my eyes except when I was a baby. However, I knew I was going to get it back someday, and I did. I always knew how to take care of myself, and I knew I did not want to depend financially on anyone when I grew up. I knew this early on as my mother was adamant about me and my sister attending college. There was never a question in my mind. I had always had a goal to attend college and graduate.

As an adult, in my search for who I really was, I found myself in Sedona, AZ, on a retreat, and it catapulted me into reclaiming a relationship with my little girl inside. My teacher, Rita, with whom I was doing an apprenticeship at the time, was leading this journey.

This was one of the first spiritual journeys that I attended, and there were so many people around me who loved me. I felt supported and free enough to be honest with all the participants, but most of all, I was honest with myself.

An assignment had been suggested for me to see my father's grave while I was in the Phoenix area. After much contemplation, I decided to fly in a couple of days early for this journey, so that I may carry out this suggestion by my dear teacher. I picked up a few of my closest friends, and we stayed at a Phoenix hotel before heading to Sedona. My friends were willing to go with me as I had a plan to finally see my father in his final resting place, where he had chosen to be buried. I was here to say goodbye for the last time.

We headed out to the mausoleum where he was buried, and it took me a few minutes to locate him. I found him near the top of a row and towards the back. I held a rose, which I placed in an indiscriminate flower holder in the middle of this structure. I turned and looked up towards the name "Goodman" on the outside of his final resting place. I talked to him and said it was sad that he never knew how to love anyone. I told him I was saying goodbye to him and would not be back to see him. I explained to him that I was working hard on breaking the cycle of abuse and clearing the family name. I thanked him for my life and to keep watching as he would be proud of me someday. The name "Goodman" would not be associated with heartache and trauma. I will use this name to help others by telling my story and supporting them in overcoming their trauma. I told him I forgave him for not knowing how to be a father and that I was releasing him.

I thanked him for showing me all the ways how not to be in life. I learned well from his shortcomings. I know he used to brag about me and my accomplishments, as I was the only person in the family who would talk to him after he left us. I am also the only one who is saying goodbye to him permanently and will never be back to his gravesite. I was done; I released him totally from my life, and as I stood in silence, a hummingbird flew in from the back of the structure right up to the name "Goodman." I knew then that my resilience had led me to become "The Shameless Warrior," and I would never look back. The hummingbird is known as the warrior bird, and I received the message loud and clear.

When I turned to walk out, I never looked back, and I had a memory of crying on the plane on the way to Phoenix. I wondered how someone as cruel as my father had been so lucky to have me as his daughter, who was so loving and gentle. I could not fathom it. Walking away from his grave that day, I knew that I was only passing through this family. He contributed to my life yet had never been a father or dad to me. Today, I cannot bring myself to call him either of those names. He helped bring me into this world, and that was it. His alcoholism took away his ability to be a proper father. The little girl inside who longed for her dad so many times would never have one until she discovered her true beloved.

During the journey in Sedona, I learned how to take back my innocence in a ceremony at the medicine wheel. I was led to the south and then to the west, where I would embrace this little girl I had abandoned many years before. The ceremony was potent, and many tears were shed for my little girl I had abandoned many years ago. This was just what I needed to reclaim my own power for this lost little girl and begin to feel the resilience that had carried me through all my years so far. I remember standing in the west of the medicine wheel, and when I turned to look to the east, I witnessed my teacher, Rita, playing the drum and singing a native song. Suddenly, I saw Mother Sarita walk toward me and embrace me. She took me in her arms, looked me in the eye, and told me, "It is time for you to use your heart, go forth into the world, and share your heart with others."

I revealed a secret I had never told anyone during that week in Sedona. It was by far the hardest thing I had done up to that point in my life. I broke down and was crying uncontrollably. I had so much shame around it. The shame dissipated quickly once I spoke the words. The release was more important than the content. I can remember the feeling of relief as I cried on Rita's shoulder. She explained to me that it was not my fault. I was a child and did not know any better. I had no reason to hold onto the shame any longer. I released it in that moment. My body relaxed in a way I had not experienced before. Such a weight lifted from me for the first time.

After I revealed this secret, I sat quietly under a tree. I dreamed about an eagle; its feathers were white, and I stood on a beach at the water's edge. This eagle swooped down, wrapped its soft white feathers around my body, and soared around the sun. It was quiet and peaceful, and I felt safe. Soon, it landed back on the ocean shore. I was wrapped in the eagle's white, downy, soft feathers, and it laid me gently down on the sand. I watched as it flew above me, promising me it would come back to visit. I felt so peaceful when I awoke.

Rita and I took a walk and ended up by a river. We sat down on a rock by the river; I had picked up a stick along the way. Someone had painted it and now had discarded it as if they were done with it and put it back into nature. Rita saw the stick and asked me if I would like to be baptized in the river. I answered with a resounding yes to that question. I had never been baptized in any church except to be sprinkled as a baby, so to be baptized in the river by my teacher that day would mean so much to me. After being baptized, I felt like I was part of this very loving group of women at that point.

After all the years in therapy, I could now see how they had set me up to do my spiritual work. I felt solid now; I experienced no dissociation anymore, and if there were any outstanding diagnoses, I did not concern myself with what they were on paper and did not identify with them. I simply took my medication that I had been prescribed by my psychiatrist at the time, and did not ask questions. I just knew I had been symptom-free of any mental illness since I met Gangaji in 1996, and I was not willing to take any chances. I only shared this information if it were important for someone to know or if I believed I could help someone by disclosing these facts about myself.

My resilience had allowed me to accept the fact that I had inherited my bipolar II tendencies from my late father (he was undiagnosed bipolar I, I came to believe and accept) and learned the suicidal tendencies and thoughts from my family when I was a toddler. I also went through a period of self-mutilation (which is common for sexual trauma warriors and physical trauma warriors) that I was willing to seek help for, and I did what they asked me to do. I was able to stop with the help of a psychiatrist. She had directed me to use markers on my arms instead of razors or other self-mutilation instruments I used, and I was finally able to stop hurting myself by following her direction. I was very willing to listen to my doctors and follow their lead. That is a positive trait and especially important to keep in mind as you work through your own personal trauma.

The downside of resiliency is that I have witnessed firsthand in others and experienced myself becoming so resilient that I did not ask for help. Someone who has been traumatized can shut down and feel that the only person that they can depend on is themselves. This leads to a problem of self-reliance and, at times, isolation. That person may go through life with the attitude that they do not need any help and can live on their own or find someone who may be broken, and spend their life controlling their environment. This can take a toll on one's physical, mental, and spiritual well-being.

This is not a contest to see who the highest achiever is or who can be the most resilient. We can seek help, be resilient, and accept help from others. This does not make us weak; it allows us to be in tune with our boundaries and practice our resilience in our everyday lives.

It was scary for me to have been so resilient as a child. I had to, or I would not have survived the sexual abuse and trauma of the alcoholic home I came from. As an adult, I maintained this resiliency, and it became a control issue in my life. I felt determined that I could do everything on my own, as I always did as a child. I experienced many difficulties in close relationships as I could not receive the love and care others were willing to give me. I missed so much as I held other people at arm's length with my control and resilience.

I had to learn that I did not have to do life alone. It was okay to accept or ask for help. I had to learn to receive love from others in my life in the same capacity that I loved them. I had no one I could depend on as a child, so I became highly resilient. As an adult, I learned through therapy how to trust people. As I worked through my trauma and issues, I attracted people who were at the same level I was in my recovery from trauma. I became better at deciphering who I could trust and who was not trustworthy.

Today, I can open my heart and allow people to help me if they are willing to. If there is no one there now, then I have my resilience to fall back on, and that is okay. I have learned not to put expectations on other people, yet I can ask for what I need from friends and family that I choose to have in my life. This includes my chosen family, who are just as important as my birth family. We cannot choose our birth family, yet we can choose a family of choice that loves us and has more in common with us.

Looking around me, I see exactly what I put out into this world. If I am in fear, then I see fear everywhere I look and in everyone. If I choose to see life through the eyes of love, I will see love in everyone, and my life will be much more pleasant.

How Resilience Can Work in Your Life

When something negative happens in your life, resilience allows you to return from that experience and be happy and successful again.

When you remember your childhood and the trauma or abuse that you endured, think of how you survived that event and what you did to overcome and rise above the trauma so that you could return to the life that you had before. Children are resilient and can recover from chaos when taken out of that situation. You may have had a place where you liked to be alone, without your mom and dad, where you felt safe and could find yourself again. This is an excellent example of resilience in children.

Think about when you were in school and you failed at something. How quickly could you recover from that failure and learn to get up and go on to the next learning experience? This is resiliency, for one must fail to keep learning.

Resiliency is the ability to work through trauma until one emerges from the darkness and into the light. People who have resiliency are considered capable of bouncing back from situations much faster and becoming themselves again.

This is a valuable trait to have when trauma or abuse encompasses your life as a child at home. When a child goes to school, resilient children can better cope with the change in environment by having more hope. They are more capable of depending on themselves and typically handle high-pressure situations more gracefully than those children who are lower on the resilience scale.

Some resilient children remain in the "fight or flight" syndrome, elevating their cortisol levels. This causes wear and tear on the body, making them vulnerable to sickness due to lack of sleep. This can also be a factor in ADD in children and cause behavior problems. If a child does not have enough sleep or increased cortisol levels, then decreased learning can become a factor.

There is a test to determine how much trauma a child endured, known as the ACE score, which is short for adverse childhood experiences. This test was developed by Dr. Vincent Felitti and Robert F. Anda in 1998. They interviewed 17,000 patients to help establish a link between childhood adversity and adult physical and mental health issues. It turns out they found a high correlation. The higher the number a person scores out of ten questions regarding childhood trauma, the more likely they are to experience poor health as they grow into adulthood. Resiliency helps to reduce the negative effects of trauma on the overall mental and physical health of the child and adults as they grow up.

I welcome you to examine the number of stressors that you had in your life as a child and how they affect your life today. Examine your relationships, your health, the way you communicate, and especially the way you feel about yourself and your life. Are you where you want to be in your life? Look at how you see the world; is it your playground? Or is it a place to be avoided? If you find yourself in a deficit in any of the areas above, I strongly encourage you to seek professional help so that you do not keep suffering alone.

We are here together to help one another, not to struggle alone. Your resilience will be uncovered, and the tools you have inside will reveal the answers you have been looking for. This will allow you the chance to work through your trauma and give yourself the opportunity to live the self-actualized life that you deserve.

Workbook Exercises for Resiliency

What does Resiliency mean to you after reading this chapter?

_____

_____

_____

_____

_____

Do you feel like you were a resilient child?

_____

_____

_____

_____

_____

How did Resiliency help you deal with your trauma or abuse?

_____

_____

_____

_____

_____

Did Resiliency ever save you from trauma? If so, when and how?

_____

_____

_____

_____

_____

Given your resilience, do you feel you could recover faster from adversity than most?

_____

_____

_____

_____

_____

Do you feel that resilience helped you succeed in your life?

_____

_____

_____

_____

_____

How can being resilient help you form healthy relationships and have safe people in your life?

_____

_____

_____

_____

_____

Meditation for Resiliency

Start by getting comfortable, either sitting up with feet on the floor or lying down.

You can have your eyes open or choose to close them.

Take four clearing breaths:

1. Breathe in through your nose, exhale through your mouth, and consciously let go of your day.

2. Breathe in through your nose, exhale through your mouth, and let go even more.

3. Breathe in through your nose and exhale through your mouth; on this breath, breathe all the way into your belly and let it expand.

4. Breathe in through your nose, exhale through your mouth, and breathe all the way down to your belly. Imagine a golden light or a root from the top of your head all the way through your body, anchoring you to the center of Mother Earth.

Now, think back to an age when you remember being resilient. How old are you, where are you, and what are you doing? Who is around you at the time?

Try to remember something that had happened in your life that triggered your resilience. Can you see the scene in your head?

Can you ask that child what they need at that moment? How does it feel to have their resiliency at this exact moment?

Take a minute to ask your younger self what they need from you. Listen and see if you can hear what they tell you.

Remember that this is the resilient part of you when you were younger, so pay attention to any feelings that you have at the age you first remember feeling resilient. Does the smaller part of you allow you to converse with them?

If they welcome you, listen and approach them, and give them what they need from you now because you could not give them that part of you back then.

If that part of you retreats as you approach, it is okay to say goodbye for now and come back to this meditation repeatedly until the resilient part of you welcomes you and trusts you.

Now, take four clearing breaths as you come back into the room, becoming more aware of your surroundings with each breath.

Feel free to practice this as often as you feel comfortable.

Chapter 6

Sacred Promise Five: SOBRIETY

Denial is Your Enemy to Freedom

S obriety is defined in two ways. One way to be sober is to not partake in the use of drugs or alcohol. The other way to be sober is when you are serious in mind. Become serious about changing your life and know that you are fully equipped to overcome your trauma. Working with this book is an example of being sober and not being in denial about gaining freedom.

If you are in denial about the fact that you must heal from the trauma in your life, then you will remain stuck. The truth is that it takes time and a deliberate effort on your part to overcome the effects that trauma has caused in your life. It will permeate many, if not all, areas of your life until you give it attention and bring it to light. I had to come to terms with my sobriety in both the physical sense, and I had to become serious about the fact that all the abuse and trauma I had survived were going to haunt me and affect every area of my life unless I made it a priority to recover and sought help for these issues.

I had so much shame and guilt, and I felt so much responsibility for my mother that I had to eventually overcome. The amount of anger I carried toward each parent I could not even begin to unravel until I was able to leave home and separate myself physically. It was at that time that I found out that none of these depressed, inadequate feelings were my fault.

What was in my control was using drugs and drinking, so I quit all these six months after I got out of college. It was at that time that I became serious about overcoming all the trauma I had endured and having a life filled with freedom.

I contemplated suicide for the first time when I was eleven after I was raped by my brother. It was during that incident that I fell silent and stared out the window while it happened. Later in life, I would find out that my warrior inside stood watch as my ego split that night so that I could survive the physical trauma.

An alter ego is when you have an alternate self, which normally has a different personality. The person is aware of this other personality or alter ego, unlike when someone has a multiple personality. When you have multiple personalities, there is a definitive split in one's personality, and the person is not aware of the other personality when it takes over. They may lose time when another personality takes over and have no recollection of what happened.

If anyone is aware of acting like another person yet still aware of their actions, they might have an alter ego. I was not fully aware of mine until I was an adult and in therapy. While in treatment, I was avoiding some key memories. My therapist asked me if I would be willing to have an IV of sodium pentothal (truth serum) so that they could ask me questions. They recorded the session. When they asked me how old I was, I stated I was eighteen. The next question they asked was my name. I promptly told them Michael.

There I was, out in the open; Michael was my alter ego, the funny, carefree kid with no care in the world. In college, Michael had no fear, drank a lot, smoked pot, and was promiscuous. Michael did not worry about consequences and thought and acted like he was 18 years old. Michael is still an endearing part of me. I embrace him inside of me with all my love and have no animosity towards him. I am aware he saved my life by allowing me to survive being raped. He allows me to be carefree and happy today. I am loving and open today due to my work walking through my trauma both spiritually & therapeutically. I sought out professionals and spiritual teachers to assist me through this process.

In addition to working with these professionals in the field of trauma, I completed many journals, created a lot of art, read many books, stayed motivated to recover, and always asked for help during my darkest times. I sought out and completed many workbooks on my own. I signed up for many workshops because that is where I found like-minded people who have helped me the most. The teachers I sought out present sources of meditation training, spirituality, or philosophy that resonate with my heart.

I always left my deep trauma work for therapists and professionals in the field, including many of my spiritual teachers. If I had not done all my work, I would not have been able to stay sober all these years. I went through times in my life when I could barely hold my head up because I felt so burdened by all the trauma I had survived. I stayed sober, went to therapy, maintained a job, and just kept showing up one day at a time. Just being alive seemed like a burden; however, I just kept going as I felt I would be rewarded for my hard work in therapy and in the rooms of my twelve-step meetings. I honestly found people who cared about me and life did get better as long as I just kept taking small steps forward.

I was working hard in therapy to overcome all the damage and gain freedom from night terrors, social anxiety, inadequate feelings, suicidal thoughts, Complex PTSD, and many diagnoses that had been placed on me that I had been made aware of. I was sad, and I was ashamed. I carried the weight of the world on my shoulders.

My therapist, Kathie, was committed to me, maybe because I was so committed to overcoming all that I had been through. I followed her lead and did what she asked me to do. If she asked me to do an assignment, I did it. If she asked me to go to a certain number of meetings, I would happily oblige. I had this knowing that if I did not help myself, I would end up like my father, and more than anything else in this world, I did not want that to happen. I despised him and he had a miserable life, not to mention he was the reason I grew up in what seemed like hell compared to what I was beginning to see of the world. This motivated me to just keep doing what my therapist and soon-to-be sponsor asked of me.

As soon as I became sober, I asked a woman I respected to be my sponsor. Shelley was her name, and she was chosen for me by my higher power who I had no understanding of at the time. She understood my depression when my feelings began to come up about three months after my last drink or drug. She was available to take my calls despite her busy job. She treated me like I was her daughter. It was comforting to know that someone loved me. I worked on my steps and did my first inventory for step four. I was hungry to feel better. However, it took time, and I learned how to be gentle and patient with myself. Shelley did an excellent job of modeling this for me.

Shelley had this look in her eye whenever she saw me or talked about me. I could truly feel how much she loved me. When she hugged me, I felt safe and loved. I began to know how it felt to have a mother that exuded that to her children, I cherished having her in my life. A sponsor is essential to have in the program if you attend meetings. I always had a sponsor when I attended meetings. I worked the steps so often that the steps began to work me. I applied them in all areas of my life. I practiced my willingness to surrender in my social, work, and family life.

Being sober of drugs and drinking and taking my recovery seriously is what saved my life so many times. I can remember when I attended my first AA meeting, I witnessed true honesty. I had no idea how to be honest with myself, and now I witnessed people being honest with strangers. I came to realize that I did not have any friends. I took hostages in my life. The people I kept around me were people who told me exactly what I wanted to hear. A loyal friend will tell you the truth, even if you do not want to hear it, and then support you through the shock of it. Recognizing honesty was the first step to becoming honest with myself. I had never witnessed honesty growing up, just lies, cover-ups, and secrets. It was such a relief to be sober and know that you can speak the truth and everyone will still love you no matter what. In twelve-step meetings, it is true, they will love you until you can love yourself.

I knew that if I had given up on my recovery and therapy at this point, I would have gone back to drinking and drugs. If I had done that, I am sure I would have hurt myself. I am so grateful that I have remained sober since 9/3/1991 and have no desire to put any toxic substance into my body.

In 1988, I was hospitalized for the first time in a psychiatric hospital and put on psychiatric meds. I went on disability for a year after I was released. I worked extremely hard during that year after I was released, and it was at that time that I understood how fragile my mental state was.

I remember my brother Gregg flew out to visit me to make sure I was okay. Gregg just asked me if my hospitalization had to do with what he did to me when we were kids. I affirmed to him that it did. I was twenty eight and had struggled so much, and I never thought I would hear him admit that he had molested me. Those words were impactful to me; they helped me finally relax and believe that I now had the right to speak up about this secret.

He contacted my therapist, Kathie, and set up a time for him to come to therapy for two hours with me. I was scared and had no idea what to expect from him. We went into her office together. I realized I was still afraid of him lashing out at me verbally or physically.

Kathie did a lot of talking with Gregg initially, so I sat there and listened. Then she pulled out an anger letter I had written to him while I was in the hospital and wanted to know if he could read it aloud. My body was rigid, and fear and anger began piercing through my veins. I felt like I might die because he would surely hate me if he read this!

Gregg began reading the letter aloud, and as I listened, it became evident that some evil spirit inside of me wrote this letter. How could so much poison spew out of me? He finished reading the letter and sat in the room, unaffected. He remained calm for whatever reason. I felt so disgusted I had written those words about my brother. I was feeling so much shame.

The therapist then began to speak to Gregg about the abuse. Interestingly, he revealed that our father had molested him when he was a child. It made sense that my father would have molested him as sexual abuse is a learned behavior and generational. A child does not know about sex at the age of ten years old unless someone shows him.

My brother apologized to me for what he had done to me. He thought he was showing me love. He was very sincere in his apology. He was not mad at all and said he would not ever be upset with me for bringing this up.

I must be honest: when my perpetrator apologized, it did not mend me or make me feel less ashamed of myself. However, it gave me a reprieve. Once Gregg had gone back home, I could reflect on the fact that my perpetrator had been honest in our therapy session that day. I was grateful, as it took some stress away because it was not my fault.

I was extremely vulnerable at this point in my life and needed extra support. Kathie would check in with me every day when I needed it. I began to feel a little safety in my life for the first time. She was willing to be supportive emotionally when I needed her. She did have healthy boundaries, so I began to learn what those were for the first time in my life. She was exactly what I needed at that time in my life.

Kathie introduced me to some great people, like Claudia Black, PhD, the author of several books such as "It Will Never Happen to Me," " Repeat After Me," "Changing Course," "Unspoken Legacy," "Deceived," "Intimate Treason," "Relapse Toolkit," "A Hole in the Sidewalk," "My Dad loves Me, My Dad has a Disease," "The Missing Piece," to name a few. I mentioned before I had gone to her house and talked about my sexual abuse for the first time. Claudia was gathering information for a book, so she had asked through Adult Children of Alcoholics meetings for some volunteers. I was so honored to come forth with my sexual abuse story for the first time for her research. I had enough reverence and integrity to have the courage to admit to my sexual abuse, as well as living with an alcoholic father. It felt cathartic now that my story was out. I was no longer hiding behind this veil of deception. It was the first time I told it to other people who were in the rooms of Children of Alcoholics meetings, and I was heard. Afterward, the hugs I received from total strangers were genuine. For the first time, I felt accepted exactly where I was, and it felt so warm to me to be accepted by a room full of strangers.

I attended a workshop held by Claudia Black, PhD in LA, and listened to her talk about her book "It Will Never Happen to Me." During her speaking, I noticed how defenseless she was, like a child. She felt innocent to me but seemed confident and safe within herself. She seemed accessible and able to express her love when people approached her. I took the chance to approach her afterward, and tears ran down my face. I remembered how I just wanted to be like her. She looked compassionate as she saw me, and I just said, "I hope I can be like you when I work through this stuff because I am at the beginning." She looked into my eyes and promised me it would get easier and that, yes, I could be like her if I kept working through my childhood trauma. She hugged me, and I will never forget the love I felt from her. She had no fear, only love to share. I took that on as a goal for myself from that day forward. Now that I had seen recovery that I could relate to in action, I would never give up hope.

Fast forward to the late nineties, and I was living in the Atlanta area, and I saw that Claudia was coming to speak at a conference downtown. I contacted her office and asked if I could be her runner. This meant if she needed anything during the day at her conference, I would be available to get it for her. I have always believed in paying my teachers back by helping them somehow. I was able to arrange this. I did not know if she would remember me; however, when I saw her on the escalator that morning, she remembered me! During lunch, I sat with her for a few minutes and let her know how grateful I was for that time I met her many years before. I shared with her that I had followed her lead, and I was so much happier in my life. She was so thrilled to hear that from me. I was so proud of myself to have made it this far and to be able to share that with her. Sitting with her, I felt like I was defenseless now and had no fear. All I had to give was love in my life. It was a sacred feeling to be able to let her know how meeting her some twelve years earlier had left such an impression on my heart.

In 1989, I moved to Atlanta, feeling positive in my healing process and ready to make a change. My sister Lynne and my brother-in-law, Paul, were expecting their first baby, so it made sense for me to be there so I could be the fun Aunt when their child was born. I had a blast with my nephews as they grew up, so I am glad I moved to Atlanta to be closer to family. I was ready for a fresh start and to climb the corporate ladder. I was around 30 years old, a perfect time in life to make a fresh start.

I began attending twelve-step meetings here and making friends. Life was going well for me. I found a new therapist, Helen, and continued to work hard on my issues. I had made substantial progress in California; however, I was about to be haunted by new trauma about to emerge.

In 1996, my life changed in a huge way. A friend mentioned that I might want to go to Satsang in Ashville, NC, to hear this spiritual teacher named Gangaji. I was ready to meet her based on what I heard. Simultaneously, I was in rehearsals for the Centennial Olympics Opening Ceremony, and they were grueling. The rehearsals were in the heat of the day, and I was ready for a break. I took a night, went up to Ashville, and went to Satsang.

I walked into this room of beautiful people, and all I felt was love from everyone. I sat on the floor in the middle of the room and took in the energy around me. There were two chairs on the stage and a microphone. When Gangaji came out, I had never witnessed so much light coming from a person. Her smile, her body, and her eyes were so lit up. She sat down and began to talk. Her voice was so soft yet gentle. She spoke of pure love, her love, and the love that exists everywhere. She asked if anyone had questions, and a few people went up and sat in the other chair. They would chat with her for a bit, and then someone else would come up. This Satsang went on for at least two hours, and I could have stayed all night.

I sat there and realized I had seen her before. She had been in my dreams. She spoke the words my soul had been wanting to speak for years. This was the first time I had ever been in a room with an avatar where I did not feel the need to go up and hug them. I was fulfilled just sitting and watching her. Love was exuding from her. When it was over, I went back to my hotel room. I had no words or thoughts for what I had just witnessed, only love in my heart and true peace. I felt like I had fallen in love with love that night, but I had no words to describe what happened.

Gangaji had mentioned she was going to Nashville next. I had picked up a flyer about it and made plans to go there. I drove to Nashville one afternoon and at a church in Brentwood, TN, Gangaji said something to me that dramatically changed the trajectory of my life. I went in for Satsang, and this time, I sat right in front of her. She spoke of the same things: love, our light, how we are born complete, how to sit with our feelings, and the love that is reflected to us in everyone and everything. At the bottom of our feelings is who we really are, and that is peace and love.

She stated there would be a small meeting downstairs afterward for about seven or eight people, and I had signed up for that meeting on the sheet before I had taken my seat. So, afterward, the chosen few made our way downstairs and sat with her. She was very candid and asked if anyone had something on their mind.

I raised my hand because I had something come to me that I wanted an answer to. She asked my name and greeted me as she intimately contacted my eyes. Her voice was so soothing and comforting. I began, "I come from an alcoholic home, and I was also sexually abused growing up. I have been in therapy for years now, and I have written about it, drawn about it, raged about it, screamed about it, and cried about it repeatedly. I cannot shake the feeling that something is wrong with me and that my light is burned out in my soul." Our eyes were locked in this gaze the entire time I spoke, and I could feel her energy. It was so warm, and I felt compassion and love from her. Her face was so relaxed and focused on what I was saying nonverbally and verbally.

Gangaji, still gazing into my eyes, answered me. "I grew up in an alcoholic home also, so I understand what that feels like. I was not sexually abused; however, I can tell you this, and you must get this. Any violation or harm that was done to your body, your mind, or even your soul never touched who you really are. Who you are is much greater than all of that and was here before anything was ever done to your body, mind, or soul. Nothing in this world can change who you really are; you are inherently born complete and have everything to survive with."

She never broke her gaze with me, and I was getting her love along with the message. I repeated part of it and asked her to repeat part of it. I did not have it; however, I remembered it enough to take it away with me.

I meditated on this statement that Gangaji had given me for just a few days, and suddenly, it was profound! I am not the person who grew up in that house! What had been done to me had not changed who I came into this life to be. I was already complete when I was born into my life on this earth. I began practicing meditation to let go of things, changed my attitude about life, and looked at my trauma in an entirely unique way. How refreshing to start to have some spiritual healing for my future. I felt relieved and began to let go of my trauma in a way I had never comprehended before.

This was a new beginning for me. I felt a connection to all things in the universe like I had never felt before. I was in my mid-thirties, in the throes of a divorce. I suddenly had the urge to put my wedding ring on my right hand and was ready to fall in love with myself for the first time. I finally began to take the time I needed to figure out what I really wanted in life.

I separated myself from any diagnosis I had and began to open my eyes to all that was around me. My heart began to blossom like never before, and this was the beginning of my true spiritual awakening, which I had only read about. My passion had deepened for the truth of who I was, and this was just the beginning of a freedom and true happiness I only imagined would be mine one day.

I was sober in so many ways, and it was paying off for me. To this day, I relive that moment with Gangaji, remember the feeling, and know that a rebirth took place that day in the downstairs hall of that church in Brentwood, TN. I still see Gangaji when I can, listen to her on social media, and always remember where I came from. Her voice to me feels like love and infinite wisdom. If I cannot sleep, I will put on my headset and listen to her calm voice as she lulls me to sleep.

Soon after I met Gangaji, I attended a seven-day silent retreat in the mountains with her. I learned so much about myself and others by being in silence for a week. I would go to the meditation room in the evening and practice, allowing my emotions to run through me. Sometimes, it took a while; however, once they were all gone, my mind would clear, and my heart would open, and there I was, sitting with my true self, with peace and love.

After this retreat, I figured that as long as I stay sober in my life, this allows me to connect to peace and love at any time. I have a far better chance of accomplishing this when I do not have toxins in my body.

I need to keep my body free of toxins and my mind clean. This allows me to feel my emotions as they arise and release them. It allows me the freedom to live in the moment and take in everything that is going on. I enjoy nature around me, the people, and the places where I choose to go.

My first spiritual experience occurred soon after I met Gangaji in 1996. It was summer, and I (along with the group I played djembe with) had been chosen to play drums in the 1996 Centennial Olympic Games Opening Ceremony. We practiced for several weeks for long hours during the day. I met Gangaji during this time, and she spoke of the oneness of all of us and how we are "all alone." She would say love brings us together; if we look, we see ourselves reflected in everyone we see. It made sense to me, and I was about to experience this.

The scorching summer night came when we took our place on the field of the Olympic Stadium in Atlanta, GA. We were on live television around the world and were the first act to perform. We were on the field in our tribal costumes that represented the colors of the rings. I was standing there, and suddenly, I felt the oneness of everyone in the universe together at that moment. I was struck by so much happiness and love that so many people were together and that no matter what was happening anywhere else, we were all together, having an experience and connected. I could hardly speak by the time we were back out on the field at the end of the ceremony. We were surrounded by athletes from around the globe together at that moment. Though we could not communicate with most of them, we could smile and shake hands and be in the same universe together. I had never had the feeling of the oneness that I experienced that night, even though I had been in crowds before that seemed cohesive and charismatic. It was an experience and a feeling that I will never forget.

This was the beginning of a time in my life that would prove to be the most influential and spiritually grounding. I was on the verge of finally coming home to who I was, and life changed for me in a way I never believed it would. I let go of who I thought I was and stepped into who I knew I was for the first time.

I knew that being sober and clean made this all possible. If I had stayed active in my addictions, I would never have experienced life as it was beginning to change for me. Being sober and clean afforded me the ability to go back, look at all my stories and agreements from my childhood trauma, and feel my feelings. Once I have felt them honestly and fully, I could make new decisions about my life and set an intention for today and how I will live my life in the future.

How Sobriety Can Benefit You

Sobriety means being serious of mind when it comes to facing the truth of what has occurred in your life. Sobriety also means abstinence from being intoxicated or using drugs to mask your feelings so that you become numb.

You will benefit from returning to the traumatic event and being courageous enough to walk through the feelings and truly feel them. Then, you can see the events objectively and make new decisions about those traumatic events and their outcomes in your life. When you were experiencing the traumatic event, your mind may have been totally shut down, or you might have been active in your addiction so that you were numb.

Now, facing the truth of what happened and walking through the "fire" to get to the other side is critical. This will allow you to take an inventory of what you experienced and offer you the ability to draft a new story about your life. You might even be able to create a new agreement about the event. An agreement can be something we decide during the traumatic event, which has caused us to be stuck at the age that it took place. For instance, an example of an agreement could be, "I was raped at twelve years of age. Therefore, I don't trust men." This is an agreement that was made subconsciously because you were raped at twelve years old, so your emotional age is stuck at the age the rape took place. Once you truly work through this traumatic event, you will be able to make an informed agreement, which may be different. It might look like this below.

"I am willing to allow myself to be around safe men and learn to trust them, even though I was raped at twelve years of age." It would be best if you determined what safe means to you in this instance. Safe may mean that they are like a big brother type of guy to you, which means they should not express an interest in you sexually and will respect you as a woman. Another indication that he would be safe is that he will look out for you, protect you against other predators, and maintain healthy boundaries as a brother would. This would involve no sexual innuendos and would listen to you when you need to talk about something as a friend would. Changing this agreement can be effective in your life, and this agreement will open your future to being more truthful about other traumatic events. This will allow you the ability to take your power back and be able to change more agreements in your life.

Your agreements will evolve and will keep changing as you grow. When you are willing to remain truthful to yourself and those around you and remain sober and clean, then you will find that you will become more willing to face the trauma from your past. You will see the benefits of facing all the trauma in your past as time goes by.

Do not deny yourself the time to work through the trauma that occurred, even if the memory is not all in your conscious mind. All memories must be dealt with for you to move on in your life.

Seek out people who are in the program, secure a competent therapist or counselor, and make sure you have a sponsor of the same sex if you are attending twelve-step meetings. This is important if you need to talk about what happened to you during your childhood or any other time in your life or just need to process everyday events.

Your life will improve once you decide to cease whatever behavior you are using to cover up the trauma. It could be drinking, smoking, using drugs, sexual relations, spending money in excess, or any behavior that is being used to avoid dealing with what is going on in your life at the present time.

If you genuinely have an issue with addictions, even if you are not excessive about it, life is easier without obsessions, and your heart will be purer with no toxins in your body. If you have a question in your mind about whether you are a social drinker or a recreational drug user, the fact that you question it at all indicates that you have a problem with that substance.

Workbook Exercises for Sobriety

What does Sobriety mean to you?

_____
_____
_____
_____
_____

Think about your life. Have there been any times when you have not been sober, as in serious, when it comes to being honest about your trauma or abuse?

_____
_____
_____
_____
_____

When you look at your drinking and drug habits honestly, have you had times in your life when you have experienced using substances to cover up the feelings of how you felt when you were being abused or traumatized? Be as honest as you can be.

_____
_____
_____
_____
_____

Have you been able to be sober, and face your pain around your trauma? Name four sensations you were aware of in your body during the trauma

_____
_____
_____
_____
_____

Write down at least one agreement that you made about life when you suffered your trauma and how you would like to change that agreement today.

_____

_____

_____

_____

_____

If you have a problem with alcohol/drugs, are you willing to seek help or talk to someone who may be able to offer some solutions around that?

_____

_____

_____

_____

_____

Meditation for Sobriety

For this meditation, please stand or sit in front of a mirror. You are going to look into your eyes.

Fix your gaze upon your beautiful eyes, these wondrous eyes that have helped you see your way through all the way to today.

Take four clearing breaths:

1. Breathe in through your nose, exhale through your mouth, and consciously let go of your day.

2. Breathe in through your nose, exhale through your mouth, and let go even more.

3. Breathe in through your nose and exhale through your mouth; on this breath, breathe all the way into your belly and let it expand.

4. Breathe in through your nose, exhale through your mouth, and breathe all the way down to your belly. Imagine a golden light or a root from the top of your head all the way through your body, anchoring you to the center of Mother Earth.

Now, breathe normally while still looking into your eyes. Keep looking, and eventually, you will see past your eyes. Take note of what you experience and see. How is your body feeling? What do you see past your eyes? What colors do you experience?

Sit there for about 5-10 minutes, whatever is comfortable, and then slowly breathe yourself back into the room.

Take a sheet of paper and write or draw what you experienced while looking into your eyes. How did it feel? Did you experience any memories? Were there any shapes or colors that you were aware of?

Just put down as much information as possible and then see if you can find any agreement that came to your awareness.

You may want to change something about these agreements. Be gentle with yourself as you experience what you wrote/drew on paper. There is no right or wrong. You are exactly where you are supposed to be, and memories will arise when the time is right.

You are free to practice this anytime you would like.

Chapter 7

Sacred Promise Six, WILLINGNESS

Participate in your Personal Healing

Willingness means to do what one is willing to do despite how you feel and are eager to do so, no matter what obstacle stands in a person's way, they will find a way to get the job done. This shows a good bit of deliberate, intentional, and voluntary ways to do the task at hand, no matter what may prevent them from accomplishing it.

Everyone has their own time in life when they finally become willing to pick up a book, make a call for help, or finally leave the situation. There is no right age when that is; the fact is, you are willing to participate in your own healing if you are reading this book.

This willingness came early for me. I read everything about psychology I could get my hands on when I was young. I was hungry for knowledge of how I was going to be able to contribute to the world when I grew up. I had always wanted to be a psychologist, so I was curious about all the different therapies available and where they were being practiced. I even had my sights set on wanting to practice at a certain clinic when I graduated.

As I became an adult and consciously knew that I intended to become a healthy and whole human, I am not sure anything could have kept me from that. I was determined that nothing would stand in my way of happiness. I was born with a fire in me that has never stopped raging to live my best life. I tend to learn things the hard way, so it took me a while to understand what happiness and freedom meant. My intention in authoring this book was to shorten the process for many of you out there who desire the same outcome.

Even with my first job after college, I made sure I had good benefits so that when something did happen to me, my insurance would cover me while I was out of work. I was unhappy when I began working but knew it would get better if I just trudged on. There was a desire to be free inside that had existed since I was a small child, and that kept me going. I did not give up until I found what contributed to my being happy and free.

I began my career in California in the mid-eighties when life was fun. I could be out about my sexuality, go to the bars in West Hollywood, and live my best life. I was also searching for the underlying cause of my sorrow and ways to overcome the pain of my childhood trauma.

In my sobriety. I stayed close to my sponsor, ticked off the days, months, and years, and collected my chips. I could not think of not drinking again for my entire life as that sent me over the edge. I slowly got the concept of one day at a time, and that was the answer for me staying sober.

Fate was on my side when I met Helen, who would be my therapist for the next 20+ years. We made an effective team as a client and therapist. I recognized myself in her and set out to become healthy, and I still believe that she loved me and put her entire heart into her work with me. I believe in miracles, not coincidences, and meeting her was nothing short of a miracle in my survival and recovery.

Helen recognized that my sexual abuse issues had been triggered in the Fall of 1990. She encouraged me to go to Sierra Tucson in AZ and take care of myself. It was the premier recovery hospital in the country for addiction and recovery in 1990, and I decided to take the time off work and go at her recommendation. It was the place that put me on my way to healing my childhood trauma by allowing me to have a safe place to land for six weeks.

I had the willingness to truly begin to face my childhood traumatic past while I was at at Sierra Tucson. We went through regression therapy, used a bataka for anger therapy, had group therapy, and they confronted us about every addiction we had. They hosted family week, where the family came in, and we confronted our family members about all the past events that had happened in our lives. I can remember my father showed up and I had a comprehensive list of events I confronted him about. He just looked at me with a blank stare. It was then I realized he was a blackout drinker, so he did not remember most of what happened when we were growing up.

I arrived at Sierra Tucson in Nov. 1990, and I was broken and scared. I was willing to own whatever I had to in order to move forward in life. I had no idea what I was doing and had never been in this situation before. I was called out for so many things, cursing to avoid my feelings and being too tough. I could not cry; I had not shed a tear in years. If they felt I might harm myself in any way, then they hired someone to follow me around 24 hours a day. She even sat by the bed while I slept. I could not figure out if they really cared or if they were just afraid that something would happen to me on their watch.

This place looked like a resort. It had an Olympic-sized pool, and we were housed in casitas with hot tubs. We walked up to dinner at the dining hall. They had equestrian therapy on-site, a labyrinth, and a Lakota Chief who taught us native traditions of the four directions, as well as a sweat lodge in which we could participate.

We had group therapy every day, several times a day, with the same therapist. I had always been an adventurous child, so I appeared tough on the outside, yet I was more like a marshmallow on the inside. I needed to be in the right place emotionally, for them to work with me to permeate my tough outer shell.

One day, a visitor showed up in the group, and she sat and watched us. It unnerved me when things were new or different, so I wanted to know who this person was. They let me know she was a supervisor and was observing. I could not stop watching her, and I wanted her to leave, so they attempted to distract me and redirect my attention back to the group. I could not take my eyes off her, and then I realized there was something about her eyes. I had never experienced this before, but I felt like she could see inside of my soul. I wanted to know her name, and it was Michael.

I found myself looking for her on campus and wanting her to return to our group. I knew I would be doing my regression work and wanted her to be there for me. What was first fear turned into trust. I felt strongly that she was safe. Something about her eyes made me feel like we connected in our souls. I found myself willing to trust that, so I felt safe enough to go with that feeling instead of pushing it away, which I normally would do.

On the day of my regression work, I did not expect much. I decided to surrender to the process and allow the therapist to guide me. I still felt tough, always making people laugh and making sure I was alone if I cried. They took couch cushions, put them all around me, and held me in. My entire body was covered, and it was dark. I was yelling that I wanted out at first, and finally, I began to hear my therapist's voice speaking to me calmly and softly. She was saying sweet things like, "You are in the womb; feel yourself inside of your mother, the embryonic fluid all around you. It is dark and safe." She spoke about how it was time for me to be born, and it was up to me to bring myself into the world.

As I listened to Gretchen's voice, I could feel my body getting smaller and smaller. The group pushed on the cushions from all directions as I regressed further back in my life. Suddenly, I felt like I was there, in my mother's womb, safe and protected from the outside world. I was content to stay right there.

Then, I was directed to begin to fight for my life as I had to bring myself into this world. I became aware that I did not have much fight in me. I lay there, and when I finally managed to get myself halfway out of the birth canal, I stopped and did not want to be touched. I was done. I looked around, and all these faces stared at me, waiting for me to fight to get the rest of my body out! Eventually, I was taken out of the womb, and I still had no desire to be touched. This was all visceral at this point; I had not been told the story of my live birth from my mother. I would flinch if someone would try to touch me. Michael came in and sat down with me, and when my eyes met hers, I was willing to allow her to touch me. I have no idea what the connection was. I felt that she was safe and would not hurt me. I was willing to take the chance to trust her, and it paid off. She held me as if I were a newborn, and it felt so good to finally feel safe and protected as an infant.

I found out I had an agreement when I came through my mother's womb that I would take care of her, keep her alive, and protect her from her feelings.

When I came into this world, my mother was traumatized by my father, and I had two older brothers. I knew it was not safe to come into the world, so I fought it as hard as I could. What happened that day in regression therapy is what happened in my actual live birth, I later found out from my mother. I was the only child of four that gave her any problems. I was lying on her diaphragm, and she could not breathe. She had been induced one time, and when she was overdue, she begged my father to take her to be induced again. He became enraged, said he would not comply with her wishes, and left her as he went to work. I know the reason I was born into that family was because I had the willingness, courage, and resilience to overcome all the abuse and trauma that occurred in that house that was directed at me. I was born with a purpose and was fortunate enough to have found my purpose. Once you learn what your true heart's desire is, then you can hone in on your life's purpose.

After that day of regression, I began to have flashbacks while I was at Sierra Tucson. They would happen randomly, and they were flashbacks of what happened to me as a small child. In a flashback, you feel as if you are right back there, and the trauma is happening to you. I had no concept of time; however, sometime later, I became aware of my surroundings again. I was on the other side of the room on the floor. It was rough, and that was the first of many flashbacks I would have. When I returned to Atlanta, they became more frequent for the next several months.

If you find yourself experiencing a visceral memory and loss of time, you might be having a flashback. It is a good idea to consult a professional therapist if you suspect this might be occurring in your life.

After returning to Atlanta, Helen saw me through my abuse recovery and sent me to specialists who were able to help me in areas where she did not have expertise. I would see the specialist for a certain time and then return and work with Helen. She was like my rock all those years, and I know she sometimes worked outside the box with me, which saved my life. She was willing to scoop me off the floor after I had a flashback and hold me. She was willing to take calls sometimes every day from me when I was feeling suicidal. She was willing to hold me and demonstrate what unconditional love feels like. She would read children's books to my inner child that I had never heard of before.

I remember her in a session in 2005; I had just returned from my first spiritual journey from my beloved Teotihuacán. I was in her office, and she took my hands as I sat before her. She closed her eyes and instructed me to do the same. I obliged, and then she asked me to tell her about my trip without saying a word. I told her all about my trip with my eyes closed and using no words. I cannot even describe the journey we embarked on that day in Helen's office. It was so beautiful and loving to come back and have someone understand where I had been and never have to speak a word. This is what my spirituality encompasses! When she opened her eyes, and I opened mine, she smiled so brightly and with so much love. She said softly, "I got it, and that sure was some journey you were on." My heart was so touched that she was able to understand my travels that I had few words to describe.

I once heard Helen tell me that I was a miracle and, by statistical standards, that I should not be alive. Over the years, so many diagnoses have been put on me that most people never live to see the other side. She stated that I had been the exception. She emphasized how hard I had worked and made it through. She said if anyone asks her if she ever had a miracle client, she always tells them my story. She is retired today, but we stay close in heart for sure.

This statement caught me off guard as I had never heard this before. I felt my sadness well up inside of me for my little girl who never had a chance. Helen had tears in her eyes as well. I thought silently about this statement and realized that she was correct. I had been labeled so many different things over the years. However, I learned that treating my diagnosis can help me heal and thrive in the world, it is not who I am. My life kept improving when I listened to the people I trust the most to help me. A good place to start is by finding and working with therapists, healers, and physicians you have faith in and do your best to follow their assignments.

There were many years that I kept taking myself off my medications, and it got me back into a psychiatric hospital. I would become depressed and confused, sometimes scared of what was going on around me for no reason. My life became so much easier once I resigned to the fact that I had a chemical imbalance in my brain and I would have to be on medications for the rest of my life. This was not my fault; I inherited this from my family. I let go of the shame and stigma around mental illness and embraced the fact that modern medicine had a way to treat my condition so that I did not have to suffer.

There are certain instances today that can still trigger a flashback or PTSD response. I stay aware of my triggers and stay away from them when possible. If it is not possible to stay away, I make sure I have a safe person with me whom I can depend on. Sometimes, I am in a situation where I must go alone, so I practice grounding techniques that help me stay present in the environment that I am about to walk into. I just stay aware of what my body and mind are telling me so I can remain calm and breathe.

Some of us may have experienced trauma before we could talk, known as preverbal. These experiences are visceral and trapped in our cells. The neuropathways are formed so early in our brains that through psychotherapy, we might not be able to break through the trauma that happened in this early stage. This is true of trauma that happens from birth to two years old or is too terrifying for us to recall. In these cases, working with child psychologists or therapists can prove beneficial. You might choose sand tray therapy, play therapy, movement therapy, or even somatic therapy to work through the preverbal stages of trauma.

While working with Helen and all the specialists she was sending me to, life started to look up for me. My career was on track, and my interpersonal relationships became something I could manage instead of avoiding. I was able to begin to release my shame and guilt, and that was a huge step in becoming willing to become a shameless warrior rather than just a warrior.

How Willingness Can Help You

Willingness is facing anything with courage, brevity, and reverence without doubting yourself. Keep persevering even if life gets tough or the process of working through your issues becomes a bit too much, and you get the desire to give up. Remember, there is a light at the end; you will gain freedom and learn to love yourself and others without judgment.

If you look at the trauma that has shaped who you are, the willingness to be flexible saved your life or, at the very least, your sanity. If you reacted the same way each time a trauma was inflicted on you, the outcome would have been quite different. The ability of a warrior to shapeshift during trauma is remarkable and shows the survival rate of all of you reading this book.

If you have picked up this book, it takes a willingness to get to a point where you are ready to act. Your life will begin to change with every step you take away from the trauma that occurred, no matter what your age.

The first day of your life begins the day you become aware enough to be willing to admit to yourself and one other person that you were traumatized or are being abused now. You are very brave, and I support you in this endeavor. Bravo to you!

Willingness is not something we are born with; we acquire it. Remember, it is your choice; you can become willing at any age. It will benefit you to admit that you are or were a warrior of trauma. This is the first step toward the willingness to be free, especially if you are currently in a trauma-filled environment.

Your individual willingness to participate in your own recovery will help you overcome the effects of trauma and move forward positively in life. By reading this book and engaging with its exercises, you are already taking steps toward healing.

There are several resources you can use to support your recovery:

- **Medical Professionals or Psychiatrists:**
  If you have any physical symptoms related to your trauma, consult a doctor. If you are feeling depressed, fixated on certain thoughts, hearing voices, experiencing flashbacks, or have symptoms of Complex PTSD, seek help from a psychiatrist or your medical doctor. They can assess your mental and chemical state and may refer you to a therapist for additional support in processing your trauma.

- **Therapists or Psychologists:**
  You may choose to see a therapist or psychologist independently to address issues like social anxiety, sleep disturbances, or persistent fears that are holding you back.

- **Legal and Spiritual Advisors:**
  You should also seek legal advice if you have unresolved legal matters or need to establish personal boundaries. Alternatively, you may want to talk to a spiritual teacher or mentor about your questions concerning a higher power or life's meaning.

- **Curiosity and Exploration:**
  It is also perfectly fine if you are simply curious about trauma and have chosen this book to assist you in working through any type of trauma.

Willingness to engage in recovery can take many forms and will vary depending on where you are in your journey.

Workbook Exercises for Willingness

What does Willingness mean to you after this chapter? How does it make you feel?

_____

_____

_____

_____

_____

Write down how you have been willing to change or let go in your life.

_____

_____

_____

_____

_____

Are you willing to do what it takes to change your life and recover from past trauma?

_____

_____

_____

_____

_____

What do you need to keep being brave and persevere through your recovery from the trauma? Where would it be appropriate to ask for help?

_____

_____

_____

_____

_____

Have you ever been willing to go to recovery and face your trauma head-on? If so, was the treatment effective for you?

_____

_____

_____

_____

_____

Are you able to maintain your Willingness to working through your own trauma?

_____

_____

_____

_____

_____

Meditation for Willingness

Gather a picture of yourself, if possible, when you were younger than you are.

Place the picture in front of where you are sitting so you can see it during this meditation.

Sit up straight in a chair, feet on the floor, and close your eyes (if you feel comfortable).

Take four clearing breaths:

1. Breathe in through your nose, exhale through your mouth, and consciously let go of your day.

2. Breathe in through your nose, exhale through your mouth, and let go even more.

3. Breathe in through your nose and exhale through your mouth; on this breath, breathe all the way into your belly and let it expand.

4. Breathe in through your nose, exhale through your mouth, and breathe all the way down to your belly. Imagine a golden light or a root from the top of your head all the way through your body, anchoring you to the center of Mother Earth.

Continue breathing normally and open your eyes when you have grounded yourself deep into Mother Earth and look into the eyes of your younger self in the picture, or picture her in your head.

Tell her/him you are willing to be there for them and that you are proud of her/him for being brave during the trauma that occurred. You are there now, and you will take care of them. Listen and see if they respond to you in any way; they might need to tell you something, or there might be tears in their eyes.

Acknowledge this. Say, "I see you, and I hear what you need, and I am here now to take care of you. Together, we can continue to be brave, walk together, and ask for help. This will result in you and I coming together and knowing each other closely."

If looking at the picture is uncomfortable, try it with your eyes closed and talk to them. That is okay if you notice they do not want to talk yet. Tell her/him you love them and are here if they want to talk at any time. Make sure they understand and know they are not alone now. Tell her/him you are a team now, and you will not leave. Tell them you love them.

Start taking deep breaths as you become aware of your surroundings. Look around the room and notice a picture or something on the walls. When you are fully back in the room, wiggle your feet on the floor and make sure you are grounded before attempting to get up out of the chair.

You can do this anytime and keep visiting your younger self to boost your little one's confidence. She/he will come around eventually, acknowledge you, and allow you to talk to her/him even if they were unwilling to do so today.

Just be patient and know they were wounded deeply during the trauma, and this was the way they protected themselves during the trauma when it happened.

Chapter 8

Sacred Promise Seven, PASSION

Desire Your True Beloved

Passion means having a powerful desire or liking for an activity or object. It can also be a devotion to a concept, such as a desire to overcome trauma. This is the way I used passion to keep moving forward and not look back. I had a fire to keep myself in recovery and a desire to live the best life possible. This passion led me to search everywhere for something I could believe in and put my faith in.

I lived my life believing that my true beloved existed somewhere out there in the world. I never thought that once I met my heart, I would fall head over heels in love with my true beloved that exists within me. Much of my life I speak about consists of the trips I take several times a year to my sacred place, Teotihuacan, Mexico.

My true passion for life began while working with Helen. She sent me to a series of therapists who were also Licensed Massage Therapists. I was not keen on the idea; however, I did trust Helen and I figured I had everything to gain. I was in my early thirties and was dedicated to a life in recovery. I felt I was gaining momentum in working with Helen. I developed a deep sense of trust with her that I had never experienced up to this point.

When a person is sexualized early in life, they feel like they were born to please everyone. I believed that if you loved me, then you must want sex from me. I had this obsession of undressing everyone I met in my mind. I was exhausted from sitting in business meetings and undressing everyone around the conference room table. This uncontrollable obsession consumed my life energy. I had no idea what touch felt like without sex.

When I arrived at my first session for massage therapy, the woman looked like a "woo woo" type of person. She took me into her healing room, where there were crystals and gems underneath her massage table. I was very naïve at this point in my life. I contemplated running at one point; however, I decided to stay out of curiosity. We sat and talked, and then she asked me to "undress to my level of comfort," to which I heard, "strip down to your underwear." I undressed to my underwear and got under the covers with my face in the cradle. She returned to the room and talked to me but never took her hands off me during the session as she massaged my back and, eventually, my entire body.

Communication is vital when you have someone on your table who has sexual trauma issues, both verbal and touching, so the person knows where you always are physically located in the room. This builds trust between the therapist and the client.

I went back for several sessions, and sometimes, I would lie on the table and cry because I felt aroused being touched. I was brave enough to tell her what I was crying about, and we would talk about my feelings. It was normal that I was being aroused as I was sexualized so early in life, and it was not my fault that I felt this way. She taught me that my body was just reacting to touch. She taught me the difference between sensual and sexual feelings inside of me. I learned what intimacy was by being honest in my communication. When I look back on my therapy, I realize that this was one of the most important specialists that Helen sent me to.

I went to several massage therapists who worked with me on bodywork and learned what safe touch was. It was so beneficial that I do not undress anyone in my mind any longer and never sexualize any relationship. Sex and Love are not related in most cases any longer for me. Intimacy, for me, is so much more profound. I can experience intimacy with others through deep and meaningful conversations from the heart.

I would much rather share intimacy with others. Sharing one's heart is so touching to me that it is my honor to share matters of the heart with others.

I learned what integrity was through working with a fantastic team of therapists and teachers. They all modeled what good boundaries looked like. I grew up in a house where there were no boundaries. I could not go to the bathroom without my brothers barging through the door. I was unable to sleep because I might be terrorized. I never brought anyone home for fear that another drunken brawl would break out in their presence. To this day, I can hear Helen in my head and heart and know what she would tell me to do in a situation, even if it would be to ask for help. I call it WWHD (what would Helen do), and having her voice in my head brings me so much comfort. She became like a spiritual mother to me and is my moral compass in life. What a beautiful, loving example of a mother she has been to me. I was blessed by my higher power to have had her and others in my life to help me locate my internal compass.

This situation is not unique to me; everyone has the people they are born to be with; you must have the passion and drive to follow hrough in finding them. Take your time to interview therapists, psychologists, or specialists before choosing a team to help you recover. The trauma of your past will continue to haunt you until you commit to resolving the havoc it has caused in your life. You must be willing to put yourself out there to begin trusting someone to make progress. Once you have passion, you will find your way back and start to have hope for your future.

After living in Florida and Colorado, my mother was beginning to advance in age. Living close to family became a priority. I was so fortunate to watch my granddaughter, Charlotte, and my mother enjoy one another for three years before my mother passed away in 2021.

When my granddaughter, Charlotte, was born in January 2018, I held her before she was two hours old. My heart was bursting with joy that my son David and his wife at the time blessed me with this beautiful, perfect angel that would be in my life forever. I felt my heart flutter as I watched her and studied every crease on her face, arms, and tiny hands! I fell in love with this little being, and she touched my heart in a way I had never felt before. Watching my stepson become a father was amazing; right before my eyes, David became this tender-hearted father.

As I sat there cuddling her in the corner of the room, Charlotte opened her beautiful blue eyes and looked at me as I talked adoringly to her. From that moment, I promised to protect her and teach her to care for herself. I vowed to always be there for her and that she would always feel secure and protected by me. I told her **#MeTooNeverYou** that night and began the hashtag on social media, symbolizing that I was going to vow to stop sexual trauma in the next two generations. I would never lose sight of that goal.

When my mother met this tiny being, she just took Charlotte from me and fell in love with her great-granddaughter within a moment. I watched my mom, who is the gatekeeper of all stories of her generation, hold her great-granddaughter, Charlotte, and realized that she was the one who taught me to love babies and children so fiercely. The two of them were inseparable when they got to visit one another. I watched as my mother always had patience and love for this little one in her own life. Here we were, three generations of women spending time together, and life was just sweet.

My mother's health began to rapidly decline when Charlotte was two years old. I had my mother come and live with me, and I was honored to take care of her for the last year of her life. She participated in our lives until the last month of her life. One blessing I was able to take advantage of by having her here was that I told her everything I wanted to before she passed away. She knew how much I loved her, how much I had forgiven my brother, Gregg, and how much I loved him as my brother.

That was so hard for her to hear that her oldest son had molested her first-born daughter under her roof, and she never knew it until I was thirty; that is when I told her. She was devastated, of course, and since I had forgiven my brother and her, I tried to reassure her that I was okay and doing well after my brother passed away in 2014.

I missed my brother Gregg. By 1997, I had forgiven myself and him. He had just been my big brother since that time. We never spoke of it again after I forgave him; I never needed to. What saddened me was that I do not think he ever forgave himself. That was out of my control, so I had to let that go and surrender it.

The forgiveness of all my perpetrators was the beginning of becoming my own beloved. Once I truly forgave myself, I felt freedom like never before and finally began to love myself completely.

I accepted myself once I truly forgave myself completely and began introducing myself as just Laura, not Laura, the incest survivor. I stopped labeling myself unless I was introducing myself in a situation where I could help others. In a casual situation, no one needed to know personal details about my life. I was okay in that moment, so there was no need to burden anyone, or bore them with information they did not ask for. I stepped into my warrior, and at the same time, I began to learn what unconditional self-love was.

My desire had led me to my true beloved within, where I met myself in true unconditional light and love. I am the light, and so are you.

How Passion Can Help You

Passion is described as having the desire to not look back and having a fire inside to keep moving forward. Passion is the desire to keep getting better and recover from whatever damage you feel you may have suffered from the trauma you have lived through.

You are already a warrior because you have survived the trauma. Now, it is your time and responsibility to have the passion to keep going and overcome anything that is holding you back in life because of the trauma you have faced.

Remember, the effects can be classified as something as subtle as sleep disturbance that may have recently started in your life. Your trauma may have stemmed from childhood and is just now beginning to affect your life. It is quite common for abuse, whether it be sexual or physical, to start to come back into your conscious memory once you are married and have children. There can be triggers in parenting your children that will bring up your own trauma from your past.

Always be honest with yourself when you are writing about your past or talking about it. You have nothing to lose; however, you stand to gain a new freedom and happiness that you have never experienced before. Look at what you used to say to people and then compare them to what you say today. Once you transition from victim mentality to warrior mode, I believe you can see how a warrior speaks as time passes. Have passion; fuel the fire in your soul to grow and recover from the trauma that haunts your past. You have the courage and reverence to stand up and face the truth of what happened as you know it today.

Passion can drive you forward even if you find yourself stuck in the past. Decide what you can change, look at your story (what happened that contributes to the way you are today), then step outside of that story, look forward, and see what story you want to create for yourself to live in today. You can dream up a life that would fulfill your heart more than trying to live out other people's expectations.

This is your life and your time to step into the light and occupy your space in this dream of yours. You will only have one life, so make it the one that sings to your heart's desire. Tap into your heart and listen to the music of the rhythm of your heartbeat. What do you gravitate towards? What grabs your attention? What is your passion in life? Find out and live it to the fullest.

Please have passion to overcome all your trauma so that you do not pass it down to the next generation. It is up to you to stay enthusiastic about your recovery from trauma so that you can finally heal this generational trauma and put an end to this familial pattern. Your children will thank you with all their hearts.

Workbook Exercises for Passion

What does Passion mean to you?

_____

_____

_____

_____

_____

Think about the word Passion and the feeling of having a fire inside you that motivated you to survive your trauma. Write about how you felt at that time. Name four feelings you had in your body.

_____

_____

_____

_____

_____

Do you feel Passion when you think about overcoming the trauma in your past and letting go of the effects they have on your life?

_____

_____

_____

_____

_____

What effects would you say the trauma or abuse have caused in your life at this point?

_____

_____

_____

_____

_____

What would motivate you to overcome the effects of your trauma if you have not started your recovery?

_____

_____

_____

_____

_____

Looking toward the future, can you name what you would like to change in your life for the better?

_____

_____

_____

_____

_____

Meditation for Passion

For this meditation, you may get comfortable lying down or sitting up in a chair.

You may close your eyes or leave them open, whatever feels safe for you.

Take four clearing breaths:

1. Breathe in through your nose, exhale through your mouth, and consciously let go of your day.

2. Breathe in through your nose, exhale through your mouth, and let go even more.

3. Breathe in through your nose and exhale through your mouth; on this breath, breathe all the way into your belly and let it expand.

4. Breathe in through your nose, exhale through your mouth, and breathe all the way down to your belly. Imagine a golden light or a root from the top of your head all the way through your body, anchoring you to the center of Mother Earth.

Now, take a couple more deep breaths, this time concentrating on your heart chakra and opening it up more with each breath. That is it. Send all your love out into the universe.

Feel the love coming back to you. Every time we send love out, we receive love back. This is an instant exchange.

Now feel your womb, which is just below your navel. Imagine there is a fire there. It will feel like warmth or passion. No story; just imagine the fire in your belly.

Feel it as it grows from your womb and allow it to meet your heart. Now, warmth and passion connect your womb and heart chakras. Just focus on that warmth. Know that this is what feeling loved feels like.

Concentrate on the warmth in your torso, heart, and womb, and know this is love. Keep up your breathing. There is no one to run to or from; it is just you generating this warmth.

You can stay with this as long as you feel safe in the warmth of the love you are generating for yourself. The idea is for your head to stay quiet; if you concentrate on your breathing, there is a good chance it will.

When you are ready, begin wiggling your fingers and toes to become aware of your body in this space and time now.

Then, open your eyes if they are closed and focus on something in the room or the ceiling if you are lying down.

Slowly and gently, bring your consciousness back into the room, still feeling the warmth of your own love. When you are ready, cross your arms and give yourself a hug.

You can practice this as much as you like to improve your well-being and foster self-love.

Chapter 9

Sacred Promise Eight, COMPASSION

Become Everything You Are

The true meaning of compassion is to suffer together. There is also a certain feeling that comes up when you witness another person suffering and feel motivated to relieve their suffering. I became motivated to heal my trauma by witnessing other people's suffering. I was ready to change the narrative from victim to warrior in the field of trauma, as we are warriors by the mere fact that we survived the trauma.

I was clean and sober and well on my way to a spiritual way of life that would add to my healing. I was working with my therapist, Helen, in Atlanta during this time, and she supported my work in my spiritual growth and encouraged me to seek out a spiritual teacher.

I kept my heart open, and when an opportunity arose in the therapeutic or spiritual world around me, I would do my best to take part in it. I was still participating in Satsang with Gangaji and keeping up with her. I was learning how to love myself and be alone in the world.

I had a great spirit brother from Sierra Tucson; his name was Lee, and he had a ranch outside of Nashville. I went to Nashville a lot and participated in his sweat lodges. I became close to that community, so I went often.

A few years after I met Lee, he asked me to come up and meet some people he was bringing to town that he felt I would like. I would not say no to a new experience, especially one that Lee, who I came to trust and love with all my heart, recommended.

This workshop was based on Don Miguel Ruiz's book "The Four Agreements," which I had read before I went to Nashville to participate. Based on the book and recommendation of Lee, I had faith in the Toltec teachers leading this workshop for the weekend.

We did some dreaming exercises that were new to me. We also did some intimacy work where we got to know one another by standing across from someone and staring into their eyes. This was different than I had ever experienced before. I could see exactly what I was feeling in this other person. It was like looking in a mirror.

We were taught about labyrinths and how to walk one by letting go of our belief system step by step. We were taught to take every step in silence and with intention. After a while, my mind was empty. I was becoming desperate to find something to fill my mind with, but I learned to enjoy the silence.

The following day, we walked in silence up to the medicine wheel on Lee's ranch, where we were asked to pick up an object like a stone. We were then asked to place all our thoughts and negative messages that came into our head into the stone as we circled the center of the wheel. I could feel the energy of the stone in my hand, the other people, and the power of the wheel itself. It was an incredible feeling for me. As we circled the center of the wheel, this time closer, I was pulled and put on the center stone, facing North. I was leaning against three other people facing the other three directions.

As I stood up there, I could feel a cool breeze blowing across my cheek, like being kissed by the spirit winds. My heart was open, and before I knew it, the people below formed a circle around us. I heard Peggy say, "Now place your right hand on their heart, open up your heart, and send all of your thoughts and prayers up to the heavens."

I felt their hands on my heart, and then I do not know what came through their hands; however, I became the light and experienced total silence and warmth. I felt like I was an eagle and was flying around the sun. Every time I circled the sun, it became warmer and quieter. The sun was blinding me, and I was aware that my eyes were closed. My heart was blown wide open, and I felt like every ray of the sun was feeding me some message with every trip I made around it. I had no human form, I was just flying like an eagle around the sun, and it was so majestic.

110

I felt like I had surrendered everything I had been holding onto in my life just for this moment. There were no words to describe what happened as I was floating out of my body and became an eagle circling the sun. There was nothing but silence as I took flight. It was as if I were sent to bring messages back to those waiting on earth. I was in the heavens as I floated above the universe. There was no doubt that something greater than me existed when I was there, and I was being prepared for it. When I returned to my earthly body, I could not speak a word. I felt it would do no justice to the experience I just had. It was as if I landed like an eagle with the wisdom of this mighty bird, yet I had to assimilate what I had experienced before I could even utter a word.

Suddenly, I felt someone support my back and sit me down on the rock, and I was leaning on someone sitting behind me. I was still being rocked around the sun, still feeling like an eagle and fully aware of the North, which is the direction of our ancestors. My body was shuttering as I tried to wake up from the most incredible dream I had ever experienced.

When I finally came back into my body, all my chakras were so open that I was hypersensitive to everything around me. When I was finally able to open my eyes, I saw the other people in front of me smiling. It was like I had been born again, and these people were there to witness my birth. It was so beautiful. I did not have any words to describe that experience.

I later realized some things that this experience at the medicine wheel intuited me, and these were:

- I was not afraid to die.

- I was no longer afraid to answer the question, "Have you ever been saved?"

- I had lost my grandmother about four months before, and I was sure there was heaven, and she was there.

- I believed in all religions.

I also knew that I could call the medicine wheel my church; however, if you took me into an organized religious church building, I would never be able to have a spiritual experience such as this.

I chose not to speak about this for two days as this experience felt so sacred to me. I had to assimilate it into my heart before any words would form about the entire experience. After several days, the only words I could put to the experience were "rocked in the hands of God."

A few years later, when I made my first trip to Teotihuacan, I learned that I was a natural dreamer. I could dream with the energy and magic of Teo easily. I had to learn how to stay present in my surroundings instead of going so far out that I was not in touch with anything around me. I was taught this dreaming technique by my teacher, Rita and picked it up easily.

Gangaji's work had prepared me for this next level of spiritual work I was about to embark on. Gangaji taught me to be present and that emotions are fluid; they come and go at any moment. She taught me that I could see her heart and love in anything if I looked into her eyes and then looked into the eyes of another person. Gangaji taught me that our true nature is love and peace.

Now, I was able to dream while I was awake, receive downloads, and not dissociate; I was able to stay present in my body. This was huge for me, as about ten years earlier, I dissociated and would not be able to dream and stay present to what was around me. There has been so much progress in my life, and I could see how much happier and free I felt!

To surrender to this dream state is where I met myself in the light; I fully embraced my heart and fell in love with who I really was. It was so beautiful to know I had been there waiting for me since I entered this life. I had never left myself; my ego had been sidetracked by life, material things, and agreements I had been taught by my parents, the school system, and the government.

This is the Toltec way of life, based on Don Miguel Ruiz's book "The Four Agreements," and was the basis for this dream work. We would look at our first attention in life, which we learned from our parents, government & education. This is also what causes us great suffering. We keep trying to live up to the world's expectations and our family's idea of what they expect us to be, and we inevitably fall short. We have no idea who we really are or what we want in our life. "Who are we really?" This question was now seared into my mind as I attended several Toltec events at Lee's rranch outside of Nashville.

All the stories I told myself about who I wanted to be, what I wanted to have, and where I wanted to go were based on someone else's expectations of what they wanted for me. Society puts so much pressure on us that I decided to overcome this suffering and decide what it was that I wanted out of life.

This is what compassion is all about. I could not have compassion for anyone if I did not have compassion for myself, overcome who I thought I was, and figure out my heart's desire. This was the early 2000s, and I began to love the people I spent time with. I also learned how to detach from my stories about the life that I lived over and over that never seemed to get me anywhere. I was so tired of feeling depressed and not being able to let go of my past. I strongly felt that with this kind of work, I was on the precipice of something huge in my life. I had no idea how my life was about to change.

There was a peace about these people that I longed for. It was not long before I began to change and feel the same peace I saw in their eyes. I began to feel like I belonged and could begin to see what my purpose was in this life.

I worked on letting go of attachments to things that I felt made me who I was. This would include my attachment to the clothes I wore, the car I drove, and even the place where I lived. I did not change any of it; it was simply that they no longer ruled my life or made me feel important. What was important began to change entirely in my life. How I felt about myself and how I started to love the people I spent time with began to matter more than anything. They were genuine friends to me and loved me with no expectations. This was all new to me and refreshing at the same time.

My heart began to feel more open, and I wanted to keep on learning more about this way of life. I felt a sense of belonging and these people were becoming my family of choice.

Gangaji had satiated my thirst to become aware of the light and love that existed in this world, and now I was reaching a new plateau in my life. I was born to discover this to recover entirely from all the trauma from my childhood. I had been in therapy for years, and now I needed just to lay it down finally, let my heart open, and be who I really was.

I was on the path to having compassion for myself like never before, and I began to love myself fully for the first time. Finally, I came home to myself.

This was the beginning of my true freedom and happiness in life, which I had worked toward for years, and now it was coming to fruition. I was unwilling to stop, so I kept bringing my stories out of the shadows and into the light. I learned early on that I had to be willing to be completely honest about every part of my life to live in integrity. Once you bring light to the darkness inside of you, it no longer has any power over you.

I was surrounded by friends willing to love me through all my darkness, and soon, I became pure light!

I developed so much compassion for myself at all ages, and suddenly, my compassion spilled over into the world for others. Once I revealed my own trauma to others and healed myself, I was able to hold space for others to have a safe place to speak about their trauma openly and heal. This is how we help one another recover from the past.

How Compassion Can Help You

Compassion is about recognizing someone else's suffering as your own. Once you can do this, you can see yourself everywhere and believe there is a better way to recover and live. It allows you to reach out to others and not lose yourself in their pain.

When you gain the ability to recognize and feel another person's pain, that person reflects what you are experiencing. You may find yourself reaching out to another person in pain or needing help, but this is only because you recognize the same feelings or pain within yourself first.

You might feel triggered by another person's pain or suffering at any given time. When you listen to others talking about feelings they have gone through or are going through, you may find yourself experiencing intense emotions and remembering things in your life that were similar to what this person is speaking about.

The best thing to do is to recognize that you have had a similar trauma experience the other person is sharing about in your personal life; therefore, hearing them share about their trauma can trigger a response inside of you. It is best to be honest with yourself and gentle with your feelings. You might experience raw emotions such as crying uncontrollably or a sudden fear of something in your life. It may manifest in poor sleeping habits, suddenly out of nowhere.

If you find yourself overcome with emotion at any time, please seek help from a professional if possible and write about it. It might just be a new memory that is surfacing from hearing someone else speaking about their trauma, or it could be that it is time for more to be revealed in this stage of your recovery. Memories will surface when we are ready to deal with them.

Show yourself the same level of compassion that you have shown other people when they revealed their trauma or you have witnessed another person telling their story. You are deserving of your patience and compassion that you have shown others in life. Be gentle with yourself and show your young parts inside the compassion you would show a child who needed comforting at the age you were when the trauma or abuse happened in your life.

Workbook Exercises for Compassion

What does Compassion mean to you?

_____

_____

_____

_____

_____

Think back in your life; at what age do you remember feeling Compassion about another person who was suffering?

_____

_____

_____

_____

_____

How does Compassion in your life help you recognize your own feelings and trauma within yourself?

_____

_____

_____

_____

_____

What qualities or traits do you feel you need help with to become a warrior of trauma instead of a victim?

_____

_____

_____

_____

_____

Can you remember anyone in your life ever showing Compassion towards you around your trauma? Either growing up or in your adulthood?

_____

_____

_____

_____

_____

Meditation for Compassion

Get comfortable lying down or sitting up with your feet on the floor.

You can close your eyes or leave them open.

Take four clearing breaths:

1. Breathe in through your nose, exhale through your mouth, and consciously let go of your day.

2. Breathe in through your nose, exhale through your mouth, and let go even more.

3. Breathe in through your nose and exhale through your mouth; on this breath, breathe all the way into your belly and let it expand.

4. Breathe in through your nose, exhale through your mouth, and breathe all the way down to your belly. Imagine a golden light or a root from the top of your head all the way through your body, anchoring you to the center of Mother Earth.

Continue breathing as you clear your mind and begin to envision yourself at an age when you were happy and doing something that brought you joy. Picture yourself back in that situation and feeling all the good feelings at that moment. Stay relaxed and keep breathing.

Remember what was going on in your life, how old you were, and who was in your life. Observe how you move about in this scene when you observe that young person. You can try to approach her/him and ask them what brought them joy at that time in their lives. Who did they enjoy being around at that time in their life? Spend some time watching how they move and see if they were laughing or if they were serious.

When you are ready to return, just become aware of your feet on the floor, your back on the floor or chair, or where you are lying if you are lying down.

Begin to breathe yourself back into your body and bring yourself back to today and your surroundings.

Make sure you feel secure and know that you are okay coming back to today.

You can practice this whenever you want to observe yourself at any age.

Chapter 10

Sacred Promise Nine, SURRENDER

Who You Are, Really

Surrender is giving yourself and your ideas to another person or something. Sometimes, for me, this was a surrender, and I was not sure what was on the other side. However, it was not going to hurt me to give myself over and find out what the result felt like. I never put myself in a situation where I did not trust the people working with me.

I have surrendered many times over the years, and each time, I was able to go deeper into my life. I surrender every day to something or a situation that comes up. I must let things go, or they drive me crazy in my mind. Surrendering can be a small thing I choose to do daily; this book is an act of surrender.

I began traveling to Teotihuacan, Mexico, with these "Toltec Teachers" or "Mystery School Teachers." This consists of teachers who take groups on spiritual journeys to the Pyramids in Teo, where the Toltecs existed between the mid-10th and mid-12th century A.D. Toltec means "Artist of the Spirit."

We spend five days going into the pyramids in Teo and doing ceremonies around our lives and stories that we grew up believing. We all have old stories that we identify with and are attached to. These stories are who we have always thought we were; however, we spend our lives trying to live up to these expectations of ourselves and always fall short. We spend time working at a job and acquiring the degrees necessary to get the material items that we believe are needed to be happy. We get our lives in order but still feel empty and alone.

This is why I went on this spiritual journey to Teotihuacan, as I was seeking a deeper meaning in life and wanted to feel more satisfaction in my life and know who I was, not who I thought I was. I signed up for this trip, and fear gripped me as I landed in Mexico City. I somehow knew my life was about to change drastically. I cried from the moment I got off the plane until that night at our first meeting at The Dreaming House in Teo, where we stayed. Each day, we would venture out into the pyramids together as a group, supporting one another in a ceremony around letting go and surrendering to the great mystery of life and learning to let go of attachment to everything in our lives. It is a dying process that takes place to who we were to meet ourselves in the light and recognize who we are.

At night, we stayed at The Dreaming House, a magical place in the village of Teo. It is beautiful and allows for a lot of creativity after a day in the pyramids. It is home to me, the food is fresh daily and it is family run. We do have groups in the evening, and they are centered around what we did during the day, how we feel, and if we could use some support about what came up for us.

In these beautiful pyramids, I have done so much of my hard work around surrender. I met myself repeatedly in the light and fell deeper in love for the first time with who I was. It was the most beautiful love affair I have ever experienced. There I was, waiting for myself to come back home.

The pyramids are very reflective of who we are. I found myself deep in thought about my life, where I had been, where I had been seeking myself all these years, and how I found myself feeling that I was home somehow in the grandiosity of the overwhelming shadows of the Great Pyramid of the Sun and the Moon. We move through the Avenue of the Dead to the different plazas, now baron and dry, where they were once lush and filled with water when the Toltecs inhabited this land. Every step I took moved me emotionally and in a dreamlike sense of where I had been in this life and all the other lives; I got a glimpse of this life and even some of the different lives I had lived or are now living parallel to this life.

The Temple of Quetzalcoatl reminded me of how I had lived my life according to what I believed I was supposed to do. I began to take inventory. I had a decent job, a nice car, nice clothes, and money for retirement with a bright future. However, these voices constantly tortured me about my worth, whether I was good enough, did I have enough, how my family and friends saw me…., and on and on. The dialogue was in my head constantly and, at times, was like torture as I attempted to gain more and more in life and became less satisfied and happy in this life.

I had looked in so many places; I had done all my hard work in therapy, I had done years and years in 12-step programs, and I was clean and sober. I worked with so many sponsors who loved me, and I did what was asked of me, inventory after inventory, which was all necessary to get me here.

There were so many questions I still asked, yet they were not necessary. All I had to do was stay in surrender and love myself exactly the way I had always been. For me to surrender fully, my life was going to come up for review one last time, and I was going to have to touch on my trauma one more time.

I had this wonderful teacher, Rita, who stayed with me as I "walked through the fire," as she called it. I was working remotely and living in Florida. I was okay at work and did not have a problem during the day. When I got off work, I would start this review of my life in my head and begin to sob and could not stop crying no matter what. I had no idea what was happening to me until my teacher became aware that my life of trauma was just coming up for review one last time and that I was going to have to surrender my life over to some new blind faith. Then, I would truly meet myself in the light!

I had no reason to believe this was what was going on. However, I had never been here before, so I had to keep going through this pain! I trusted her, so I followed her guidance even though this pain was so deep. I recognized the trauma, sexual, verbal, and what I witnessed. However, another layer was coming up for me this time. I felt abandoned, and I felt it at my core. I realized no one was there for me, and this time, in review, I really felt it. The facts were that I had been very well taken care of physically. I was fed and dressed well, and at the same time, my emotional needs were impossible to satisfy as an infant and child.

As I was dealing with my life in review, there was a conference call every week for those of us who went on the Teo journeys. I was desperate for a connection. I would get on these calls, and I could not help but cry because I was just feeling the connection with like-minded people. Each call had a random teacher and every time I would ask a question, it seemed like they would always say to me, "Keep doing what you are doing, Laura. You are walking through the fire, and you will come out on the other side." I held onto that statement, and it got me through the weekends.

During the week, Rita met with me nightly on video calls, and I would just cry, though I listened to her advice and was doing what she asked me to do. One night, I was on a call with Rita and said to her, "I don't even know who I am anymore!" I heard a voice answer that question from the other end of the computer, which shocked me, as Rita said, "Now we are getting somewhere!" I was so perplexed in that moment that I stopped crying and uttered a confused "What?" I felt that this was ridiculous. How could I not know who I was? I listened as Rita explained to me that she had never seen anyone go through as much fire as I was walking through and not come out on the other side, knowing true freedom and happiness.

That gave me the confidence to keep up the work I was doing at that time. I made a quick inventory in my mind; I was not depressed, however, I cried every day after work. I began doing my writing vigorously, and it revealed a lot of important points about my trauma that I needed to accept and surrender, so I could put them in the past for good. I really needed to die to these memories to create a new life.

I remember that my heart hurt so bad because I wanted my mother to rescue me, hold me tight, and tell me everything was going to be okay. I can remember screaming this over the phone to Rita one night out of pure frustration. This was a new level of pain I had not experienced before. Suddenly, I heard this comforting voice on the other end of the phone as I heard Rita say, "I know you do, Laura. I am here, and it is going to be all right." From that point on, I decided to trust Rita, and she never let me down. She kept pointing me to my own resources inside and taught me how to love myself and be the mother and father my little girl needed.

I remember being shamed by my mom when she once opened a letter I wrote to an older girl who babysat for us. It was about something sexual that I did with a boy in eighth grade. I asked my mom to mail it, and she chose to open it and read it. She shamed me so badly about the sexual incident that I felt ashamed of myself for years after that.

My mind just kept flooding with all this shame and abandonment. I was sure I would never stop crying. I wrote journal after journal about all the events that were coming up.

Rita had experience with sexual trauma, so I was in capable hands. I was so vulnerable, and at times, I could not figure out how to talk to people about ordinary things in my life. She helped me discern what to say and who was safe to talk to during this time.

My next journey to Teo with Rita was so revealing. I learned so much on this trip, and it was unbelievable how much I had changed since the previous trip the year before. I was making notable progress, which was obvious to others from the outside.

I have a memory of Rita talking to us on the first day in the pyramids. She said, "Look around you and notice what you see. Feel the breeze on your face and the warmth of the sun and savor this moment. You will never get this moment back." I just started to cry. The tears rolled down my cheeks and fell onto my red shirt I had on that day.

I was then pulled from the group to be a witness. Each woman came up to me and told me, one by one, about the sexual or physical trauma they endured. I was supposed to maintain eye contact with them, listen to their words, and then say, "It was not your fault; you were just a little girl. I forgive you."

This was powerful for me as I realized I was not the only one who had been sexually traumatized, and I felt so empathetic towards the other women. It was a real lesson in getting out of myself, focusing on others, and helping them through their pain.

It was so powerful to be there for others and to surrender my own pain. I could feel my pain, and during that week, it became something I began to understand.

I came to understand that giving to others was a way to surrender all of me to the moment. I learned to open my heart and share my love with others, knowing that I could raise the vibration of this planet.

On the last day of our journey, we took a tour of the Basilica in downtown Mexico City. The cathedral on Tepeyac Hill is the original temple built for Mary of Guadalupe. This was my first visit, and there were statues of the Archangels out front. One of them is Archangel Michael, the protector.

When I first saw the statue of Michael towering over me and Mexico City, I began to weep uncontrollably. At first, I could not understand why; however, as I cried, it became apparent why Michael meant so much to me.

That little girl that was being raped at eleven years old, who was staring out the window, identified with the name Michael because the archangel Michael had rescued her that night. As I stated earlier in this book, Michael was my 18-year-old alter ego.

As I stood there crying, I realized that Michael had been born with me as an infant and had protected me all my life. Michael and his energies have always saved me from being harmed, gave me the courage and reverence to make it through all the trauma and gave me my shameless warrior spirit.

I surrendered my life that day to my faith when I met myself there in the light at the top of Tepeyac Hill with Archangel Michael. From that moment, I knew that I could embrace little Laura and Michael inside of me and be whoever I wanted to be at any given moment.

I glowed from the inside out and knew I would be okay. Freedom and total happiness were now in my life from that moment on. I had now come full circle in my spiritual life, met my heart, and fell deeply in love with my beloved.

I define surrender as having faith in something, even if it is blind faith. I am now in the habit of surrendering to blind faith, and I accept whatever faith must teach me from the experience of just handing over my power to someone or something, even if I am not sure of it. I always make sure that I am in a safe environment before I surrender. That way, there are safe and competent people around, and I am protected. Once you tune into your heart, you will know when you are safe and trust your heart to let you know.

When I surrender my life to a new experience in a spiritual place, I have always learned something beneficial when I come out on the other side. There was a time when I needed someone to be there for me on the other side; however, now I have learned how to be caring and loving towards all my small parts inside. This has caused me to be more open to surrender and have compassion for myself and others.

One act of compassion towards myself I have learned is that if I cry, I allow myself to cry until I cannot cry anymore. I let my heart break open. I am okay, and crying will not hurt me. Once I am done with the tears, I lay back, stretch my arms out, and take a deep breath. I can feel how much room there is inside of my heart for the light to come in. I close my eyes and imagine all the people who love me. I pull their energy into my heart, and I feel so loved. It is one of the most self-loving and beautiful things I do for myself. It reminds me of how many people genuinely love me unconditionally.

How Surrender Can Help You

Surrender means to give yourself over to an idea or a program to improve your life or make yourself a better person. Look at your life and take stock of the things you hold on to. Are they permanent? Or can they be taken away instantly, such as a job, money in the bank, a particular car, clothes, and more? Now imagine yourself without those nice materialistic things in your life. How would you feel about yourself and your life?

Do you believe in a power that is stronger or higher than you that can hold your feelings or trauma that might come up in your consciousness in your lifetime? Once the job, money, car, clothes, or even status disappear, is there something you believe in? Is your EGO tied to the job, money, car, or clothes? We are all aware that EGO = Easing God Out. This includes a God of your understanding.

Even if you are in 12-step programs, do you have a sense of a higher power, or are you an atheist? None of these concepts are right or wrong, good or bad; they just are.

Look at your life; there is no right or wrong answer to your beliefs about a higher power. You are free to choose whatever it might be. It helps if you can surrender your feelings, your situations, your trauma, or anything that is in your mind over to something, even if it is a box with a label on it ie...a "feelings box," (make sure parentheses are going the correct way on "feelings box") "god/goddess box," or whatever you choose to call it. You can write down what you want to surrender on paper, put it in the box, fully surrender it, and let it go completely.

This way, you can clear your mind to be more productive in your current life. When you get overwhelmed in life, consider meditating or praying to a power greater than you and turning your troubles over to that entity. You will find peace in life if you are willing to let go completely of all that burdens you.

If you live in this moment only, you will not be overwhelmed by what you must do later in the day, tomorrow, or in the future. Life becomes simple once we surrender our sense of time. Break your days down into steps, and the simple things in life will become special again. Stop and look around and feel the sun on your face, the wind in your hair. You will be brought back to this moment, and life will be beautiful again.

My first spiritual teacher, Gangaji, taught me to meditate, and when we asked her what prayer was, she answered meditation. Sit with your thoughts and feelings and allow them to dissipate, and you will find the true essence of yourself, which is peace and love. Remember, when you are burdened in life, look around; you will see fear in the world. Try to sit and meditate, and you will find the love that exists in all of us. Once you surrender to that love inside your heart, you will only observe love all around you in the universe.

Surrender is the letting go of anything that does not serve who you really are. This will simplify your life and allow you to live in the moment.

Workbook Exercises for Surrender

What does Surrender mean to you? What does the action of Surrender feel like and look like to you?

_____
_____
_____
_____
_____

What is your understanding of Surrender, and have you ever surrendered to a program or any person who could help you overcome trauma?

_____
_____
_____
_____
_____

How would you describe your relationship with a power that is greater than yourself? If you do not believe in a higher power, write about that.

_____
_____
_____
_____
_____

Do you believe that you would be able to Surrender, given the trauma that you have endured?

_____
_____
_____
_____
_____

Do you believe that your true beloved is inside of you? Would you like to meet her/him and be able to experience true self love?

_____

_____

_____

_____

_____

Do you understand how to fully Surrender to an experience? Write about what blind faith means to you.

_____

_____

_____

_____

_____

Meditation for Surrender

Sit in a chair with your feet flat on the ground.

You may close your eyes or leave them open.

Take four clearing breaths:

1. Breathe in through your nose, exhale through your mouth, and consciously let go of your day.

2. Breathe in through your nose, exhale through your mouth, and let go even more.

3. Breathe in through your nose and exhale through your mouth; on this breath, breathe all the way into your belly and let it expand.

4. Breathe in through your nose, exhale through your mouth, and breathe all the way down to your belly. Imagine a golden light or a root from the top of your head all the way through your body, anchoring you to the center of Mother Earth.

Take yourself back in your mind to a time when you were with a person who felt safe, someone that you trusted with all your heart. Imagine that this person is with you today. What would you say to this person if you could talk to them about your trauma that happened? What would you ask them for? It could be as simple as a hug or a shoulder to cry on, or you may want to surrender to them and ask them to help you out of the situation or for advice on who to see as a professional for help.

If you are not ready to surrender anything, you can just imagine this safe, trustworthy friend or loved one is just spending time with you.

Take your time with this person, and when you are ready to come back, tell them thank you, and you will be back to keep the line of communication open.

When you are ready, wiggle your hands and feet to establish a connection with the room you are in. If your eyes are closed, begin to open them and focus on something in the room. Look around slowly so you can remember where you are today.

Use this meditation when you would like to visit someone safe in this day and time or from your past. It will help you when it is time to surrender and ask for help in your own recovery.

Chapter 11

Sacred Promise Ten, SPIRITUALITY

Embrace Your Authentic Self

Spirituality comes from the Latin word spiritualitas, the derivative of the noun spiritus, meaning "the breath of life." In English, spirituality comes from recognizing a feeling or sense that there is something greater than me. This means greater than being human in a sensory experience and the whole of which we are part cosmic or divine in nature.

Gangaji describes to be awakened in spirituality, "The spiritual path is a path of death, a path of loss. In the willingness to lose everything, the recognition of who one is has to be revealed." She was the first to describe what my soul had waited my entire life to hear. I began to die to the idea of who I had known myself to be in this world and began to awaken to who I was. I learned from Gangaji that suffering was optional and that peace and love were my true nature. I started to see myself in her eyes, which translated into seeing love in everyone and everything. I was willing to die to live, finally.

Every day, I would wake up more aware of my surroundings than the day before. I was more in tune with the idea that I could be free and happy if I were willing to let go of all my old ideas. I learned that love has nothing to do with another person; love reflects how I feel about my soul inside of me. Love became truth, truth became self, and to surrender to the truth of myself was to surrender to love.

I began to respect my body as a temple and continued not to put alcohol or drugs in it daily. I decided not to participate in living on the edge behavior. Once I discovered Gangaji, I stopped riding motorcycles and no longer participated in what I believed was risky in my everyday life. I wanted to live every minute I had to help others who had gone through trauma and love them the way I had been held in my journey so far.

I know that all my old stories served me well during the trauma that I had lived through. The agreements I made allowed me to stay safe, look into the future, and know I had a way out as I grew up. Once I got out of the house, I exhausted myself, attempting to live up to all the expectations I had for myself. I lived my entire life in fight, flight, or freeze.

Due to being molested so early in life, I have never felt pure or untouched. For this reason, I could never call myself a virgin. I always felt shame and guilt for something I had no responsibility for. I was a small child when it began and only eleven years old when my main perpetrator, my oldest brother, moved on with his life. I never had a sense of my own identity because I was shaped by sexual acts that changed my personality during my developmental years.

I struggled with this and could not embrace myself as a whole woman until 2015. This had left me with a lifetime of failed attempts at sexual relationships with women and men. I went on a journey to Teo with my teacher, Rita, and this healing would allow me the purity I had longed for.

One of the pyramids is the Temple of Quetzalcoatl, which translates to "Feathered Serpent." He was one of the most important deities in the Pantheon of Mesoamerican culture. He was worshipped by the Toltecs and the Aztecs and embodied duality, symbolizing both the physical aspect of the serpent and the spiritual aspect of the feathered bird. He existed from the underworld to the earth, all the way to the upper world. In mythology, he was the double-headed feathered serpent spanning the underworld to the heavens.

Quetzalcoatl is a powerful symbol of how the underworld rises to kiss the heavens and all that exists in between. Entering the temple itself is an extremely sacred and powerful experience.

It was time for me to experience the miracle that Quetzalcoatl had in store for me on the last night of our journey in 2015. This would change me on a deep level, one that would finally set me free to embrace who I truly am spiritually.

We entered the cave under the cover of night when the moon was high in the sky. This was an all-women's trip, so we filed in by the light of the moon that was watching over Quetzalcoatl.

We were led into a cave entrance by flashlights underneath the temple. As we arrived at the center, it was evident that there were four tunnels, one from each direction, that met in the middle, which opened to a small cave-like room. We settled there, all the flashlights were turned off, and we were left to proceed with our meditation.

In hindsight, I know the ceremony was done on my behalf as I was at a turning point in my life. I was on the verge of embracing who I was and loving myself fully or going home on the precipice of a huge awakening. I am positive my teacher, Rita, had witnessed a spark in me earlier in the week when we were at the temple of Quetzalcoatl. This is why I found myself back here, feeling so energetically charged and on the verge of something spectacular about to happen.

I can barely speak of what I felt that night in my body. I never doubted miracles exist; however, I can honestly say I have never received such a gift so divine and sacred that it defies any mystery ever explained in any book or even spoken about.

What I experienced can only be transmitted energetically and with so much honor and respect to the ancient spirits that were called in to assist in the healing. The heart and vessel that channel these spirits in must call them in with such reverence and love, and the healer must be impeccable and have a clean mirror to work with as the energy passes through their physical channel to the womb of the broken or sexually abused. There was a disconnect between my 1st and 2nd chakra due to the sexual trauma that needed to be healed in my womb.

What took place in my body defies anything short of returning me to my innocent, sacred divinity. My teacher, Rita, stood in front of me and turned me in the direction of the Angel of Death. Then, with laser-sharp precision, she directed the energy of Quetzalcoatl into my womb between my 1st and 2nd chakra. Though it was pitch black, I was aware of her standing in front of me. The energy was so intense and precise that it almost burned me. It felt like it was burning out the wound and returning me to a whole person for the first time since I came into this world.

I felt this wave of energy begin to pulsate my body, and I went into a trance-like state as Quetzalcoatl began to move through all of my chakras. My energy was open, and I felt a deep cleansing begin to take over my entire body. My eyes were closed, and I was making guttural sounds as the cool ground of the sacred cave sent waves of an energetic cleanse through my ethereal and physical body.

I knew that women would gather in caves to perform healing on one another in ancient times. To be nestled in Quetzalcoatl's feathers as I was being returned to my innocent, virgin-like state was nothing short of being back in the womb in embryonic fluid again.

I felt the waves of purification wash over me repeatedly as my body rocked to the rhythm of Mother Earth. I could feel my energy and temperature rise and begin to erase every single thread from every incident of abuse that was ever bestowed upon my body during this lifetime and any other.

The power would not stop; every memory was taken away as if brand new neuropathways were formed for the first time. Waves of passion took over my sacred body as this soft-plumed serpent breathed his fire in and out of my womb, cleansing me and purifying every fiber of my being. There is no doubt I was given a second chance to live for once in this world and experience this amazing feeling of what it feels like to be whole.

I was surrounded by women in this dark cave who loved me, and I felt the angels around me just holding space for me as my body was being wrung out. In my dreams simultaneously, I saw myself inside Quetzalcoatl's soft plumed feathers of her belly as I experienced the sensation of being pure in mind, body, and soul.

My innocence was being returned to me; my body felt renewed, as if no one had ever touched me against my will, sexually or physically. I felt a burning in my vaginal area as if it were on fire one last time; the toxins were released as I began to stir in the serpent's belly on the cool ground supporting me.

I could feel Mother Earth supporting me as I returned to the world in total darkness. I had no words to say, no need to utter a sound. I only felt love for the little one inside me, who had never felt 100% whole until this moment. I met my true beloved, and she was much younger. At that moment, she had been there waiting for me all my life. I hugged myself as I sat up, aware of how sensitive my energy field was to everything around me. I was afraid that another person might interfere with my energy.

As I stood up, I felt off balance. Rita took my hand in the darkness and led me out of the cave. While everyone else piled in the back of the pickup truck, I sat in the cab next to

Rita, as I needed to feel safe and protected in that moment. We never spoke. I stared out the window at the moon over Quetzalcoatl that night, which is now etched in my memory as we drove away. I remember looking up at the Avenue of the Dead as we drove away and staring at the Pyramid of the Moon, standing majestically against the moonlit sky.

I had just met my youngest true beloved and fallen in love with her for the first time as I fell into the wholeness in my body for the first time in my life. I felt like a virgin, which had always been my birthright yet was snatched from me sometime after I came into this world. I no longer felt violated at all. I felt purified and now knew I could embrace the totality of who I really was.

Before I was born, I was always my beloved and who I really am. Today, I know all the secrets from six generations in my family and have openly talked about them so that I may heal them. My father abused my brother; my brother abused me. A great uncle abused my mother. I refuse to stay silent any longer about my family. It stops with me. **#MeTooNeverYou** Now that I knew who I was, I knew I had always been there, waiting patiently for me to come back and meet myself in the light. There I was in that truck, feeling small, sitting next to my teacher, not crying, just feeling vulnerable at that exact moment because I had finally met my innocent child and could now love her and care for her the way she always needed to be cared for.

I embraced my innocent child inside and became the benevolent mother and father she never had, and it grounded me like nothing before. I am free and never lonely because I am here to nurture that innocent child who was abandoned so long ago by me. I can now close my eyes and pull in the energy of whoever I want to be with at any given time. I learned so much about loving myself that night: how to open my heart, receive love, and not be afraid anymore.

Today, I know that my most important traits are humility and vulnerability because, without those, I am not capable of loving or receiving love.

My purpose in being here is to help you overcome your trauma and to create a safe space for you to be able to talk about your story. Then, you will be able to recognize that your shame is not yours to carry, and you can release it and become the shameless warrior that you have always been!!

I have committed my life to locking arms with all who have gone through trauma or will go through trauma so that we may heal and end this tragic childhood nightmare by providing a safe place for everyone to heal.

How Spirituality Can Help You

If Spirituality means believing that something larger than you exists in this universe, it can help you turn your sorrows and woes over to a being that can handle all you are willing to surrender.

This is not to say that God is the only sense of spirituality one must consider larger than yourself. I have heard of great spirit, universal love, dharma, nature, mama pacha, buddha, etc.

When you were young, there was a good chance that religious practice or belief in a higher power was dominant in your household. If you experienced trauma in this household, you may find that you disbelieve in the very spiritual deity that you were taught to believe in.

It can be referred to as spiritual abuse if the religious or belief system was forced upon you, and the adults were not living by the morals and standards of the belief system that they were instilling in you. You may find that your parents would drop you off for a religious upbringing or send you to a school of a particular deity while they practiced no religion at home.

When trauma occurs, especially during childhood, you may feel abandoned when you seek help from a higher power, particularly in moments of desperation. As children, we often do not understand that prayer or asking for divine intervention does not always work in the way we expect. Without guidance or support to help make sense of what prayer or meditation involves, many adolescents or adults may grow up to reject the idea of a higher power altogether.

To embrace a higher power capable of handling all our problems, we need to be willing to re-examine the beliefs we formed during trauma, especially those beliefs developed during our formative years.

Children who can connect with a higher power or a spiritual deity often have a greater chance of healing with fewer lasting wounds. In contrast, if you internalized guilt or shame as a child, you may have felt that something was inherently wrong with you. A religious or spiritual practice can provide a foundation for understanding how to turn to a greater source through prayer or meditation. This foundation can offer an advantage over those from environments where spirituality is ignored or dismissed or where the individual is taught that they themselves are the highest authority.

Reflecting on your childhood, consider whether you were taught to surrender your worries or problems to a higher power. Ask yourself if that higher power or spiritual framework still resonates with you today and whether you continue to have faith in it to help you handle your troubles.

You can explore diverse types of higher beings, religions, or even non-religious deities and see if you can find one to put your faith into. There are so many available that you can try to see if you can surrender your troubles to that higher power. It is comforting to know that somewhere, something can handle all your anger, resentment, and troubles when you are in a time of need.

Meditation and prayer work. As Gangaji says, "Peace is our true nature." If we all strive to live in our true essence of peace and love, think of how much we can heal ourselves and love others.

And so it is…..

Ometeotl

Workbook Exercises for Spirituality

What does Spirituality mean to you? How does it show up in your life?

_____

_____

_____

_____

_____

What type of Spirituality were you raised with as a child?

_____

_____

_____

_____

_____

Did you believe there was a deity that was higher than you as a child? If not, describe why.

_____

_____

_____

_____

_____

During the trauma, did you use meditation or prayer to deal with the aftereffects of the trauma?

_____

_____

_____

_____

If you are not spiritual at all, do you believe practicing meditation or prayer might benefit you?

_____

_____

_____

_____

_____

Have you tried eastern types of Spirituality to see if it might work for you?

_____

_____

_____

_____

_____

Meditation for Spirituality

Before you begin, have a pen and paper or art supplies and paper ready beside you to utilize once you are done with this meditation.

You can either lie down or sit in a chair with your feet flat on the ground.

You can do this with your eyes open or closed, though this one may best serve you if you feel safe closing your eyes.

Take four clearing breaths:

1. Breathe in through your nose, exhale through your mouth, and consciously let go of your day.

2. Breathe in through your nose, exhale through your mouth, and let go even more.

3. Breathe in through your nose and exhale through your mouth; on this breath, breathe all the way into your belly and let it expand.

4. Breathe in through your nose, exhale through your mouth, and breathe all the way down to your belly. Imagine a golden light or a root from the top of your head all the way through your body, anchoring you to the center of Mother Earth.

Think about what makes you feel safe in the universe and see yourself there.

See an image of yourself there. Is it at the ocean? The mountains? In an airplane? Or picture any place where you feel safe. Is there a specific person that is with you? Or are you alone in this safe place?

How do you feel being in this safe place? Do you feel as if something or someone is protecting you even if you are alone? Or do the safety and protection seem to come from within you or from another person who may be in this place with you? Breathe into this space and relax further.

Now listen to the sounds around you in this safe place. Are they nature sounds? Or is there some voice that is speaking to you that does not belong to anyone who is with you. Can you identify this voice? Does it seem to be coming from a higher self or being? Is it supportive and loving? Take note of anything unusual about your surroundings or familiar about them. Be aware of any subtleties that may be present.

Now, breathe deeply again as you come back into the room you are in. Feel the chair or surface you may be lying on with each breath.

Open your eyes slowly and become aware of what is around you, remembering where you just came from in this meditation.

Once you are back in your body, please pick up a pen and paper or art supplies and begin to write or draw what you experienced in this safe place and how it made you feel. Include all the details you can. See if you can determine if it was a higher being that you felt safe in the presence of or if it was yourself or a specific person in your life.

There is no right or wrong situation here; this is merely an exercise to see if you can determine if there is a specific place that you put your faith in.

About the Author

Laura Goodman is an author, CRS, Treatment Consultant who lives in the metro Atlanta area. She is available to Facilitate Workshops, Mentor and do Speaking Engagements based on her personal recovery from addiction and trauma. She has been clean and sober since 9/3/1991. She has apprenticed with many spiritual teachers for the past 25+ years. She has done her own personal recovery of 35+ years in therapy. She now works in the treatment industry, where she does interventions, case management, as well as treatment placement.

Laura worked in IT for 25 years and now plans to spend this part of her life living her life's purpose and being in service to as many people as possible.

You may contact her at.
theshamelesswarrior@gmail.com

Or visit her website.
https://www.theshamelesswarrior.com

About the Author's teacher Rita

Feel free to reach out to my spiritual teacher, she is a wonderful, endearing mentor that taught me to love myself unconditionally. I was able to forgive myself fully and fall in love with my true beloved because of this selfless human. She has contributed to me coming fully into my authentic self over the years. I love her dearly.

Rita Rivera Fox
Transformational Coach & Mentor

Ritariverafox@gmail.com

http://www.ritariverafox.com

310-869-5018
Boulder, CO

www.ingramcontent.com/pod-product-compliance
Lightning Source LLC
Chambersburg PA
CBHW080822120626
46556CB00010B/3355